Joyful Together

Joyful Together

Joyful Together

Using Everyday Moments to Build a Loving Relationship with Your Child

Holli Ritzenthaler
Georgie Gray
Michelle Wallace

Benjamin Kearney, PhD

THE INSTITUTE OF
FAMILY & COMMUNITY IMPACT

An OhioGuidestone Company
Berea, Ohio

The Institute of Family and Community Impact
An OhioGuidestone Company
www.OhioGuidestone.org

ISBN 978-1-951211-05-9
Printed in the United States of America
1

Contents

Preface

by Benjamin Kearney, PhD

The concept of toxic stress is relatively new to the fields of psychology and human development. Only in the last twenty years have researchers begun to understand the long-term impact that adverse childhood experiences such as poverty can have on neurobiology, general health, and even life expectancy.

But what can we do about it?

There are effective, evidenced-based protocols for helping people with toxic stress. They typically involve ten or more weekly hour-long sessions with a clinician. Parenting classes can demand an even greater time commitment. But this is a lot to ask of families that are already struggling to meet basic needs with little or no support. As we communicated with peers across the state, my colleagues and I at OhioGuidestone saw the need for more options.

Thanks to the pioneering work of neuroscientist Dr. Jaak Panksepp, we know that children need lots of care and play in their lives in order to experience joy. We also know that joy is the greatest antidote to stress. And while traditional play therapy can be beneficial, it requires preparation and toys and yet another demand on a family's time. So I asked the therapists at OhioGuidestone to brainstorm a new approach to tapping into the power of play, a series of brief activities that families can use anytime, anywhere, on a schedule or spontaneously, to bring more joy to their lives.

Based on their decades of experience working with families in Cleveland and its inner-ring suburbs, their extensive clinical reading, and their personal experiences as parents, they began creating activities that would appeal to kids and caregivers. The families they work with helped them test and refine the activities, and the therapists watched as the energy changed. Rigid, rule-bound parents relaxed. Angry, distrustful children were able to giggle and enjoy connection. And they were eager for more. The laughter alone showed the therapists that they were onto something.

We decided to call the process "Joyful Together".

There is a great deal of science behind Joyful Together, but no one needs to understand any of it to engage in the activities. Indeed, the science just confirms what most people instinctively know: That joy is a light that can guide us through darkness.

Families will continue to face challenges; stress is an unavoidable part of life. But we believe that Joyful Together activities can help families turn everyday moments into opportunities to recharge and, ultimately, to develop stronger, closer, more resilient relationships.

Introducing Joyful Together

As a parent, have you ever felt like you just can't handle one more whine, one more debate, one more tantrum, one more "But *whyyy...?*"

You aren't trying to lasso the moon. You just want your kiddo to get dressed. Do a little homework. Maybe eat a sprig of broccoli, or something remotely resembling a vegetable.

Then have you worried, in a frazzled moment, that maybe your response isn't making things better—and might even be making things worse? *Am I an awful parent? Am I ruining my child?*

If so, you're not alone, of course. But...

What if you had a magic tool for gaining your child's cooperation?

What if you had a superpower that could brighten your child's mood? Your mood?

You do.

The magic tool is you.

The superpower is your ability to make a playful connection.

This book will tell you how to unleash that superpower to build a stronger relationship between you and your child—and prepare him or her for healthier long-term emotional development.

It isn't really magic, of course.

It's even better: It's science!

The simple relationship-building technique we're going to introduce is based on extensive research into how our human brains function, especially during childhood. Hundreds of thousands of years of evolutionary biology are involved, complex chemical interactions, neurophysiology...

We'll describe some of that science, but you don't have to understand it to use it. You'll just see it work.

Best of all, you can use your newfound superpower with any age child, almost anywhere, almost any time. It costs nothing and requires no special tools or training, just you and your child and a few moments together.

We call this relationship-building technique "Joyful Together." It uses simple, everyday, joyful experiences between parents and children to build a foundation of safety and love. It benefits children and parents equally.

We translated dense research into practical, fun, easy activities that you and your family can use today to strengthen your relationships for a lifetime.

What is joy?

Everybody knows what joy is, right? Happiness and blue skies! Puppies and kittens!

Well, that's one way to describe it.

Another way to describe it—neurophysiologically speaking—is this: Joy is a euphoric experience that leads to many positive body, mood, and behavioral changes. It's your brain and body working together. When you experience joy, natural chemicals in the brain flood the body, and as a result, you feel happiness and calm, even bliss.

The benefits are both immediate and long-term. Even just remembering a joyful moment from your past can cause your body to respond on a chemical level. (Try it! Recall a joyful memory and see what happens.)

Joy changes your brain and body for the better.

Why "together"?

Sure, we can feel joyful while alone.

Your child can feel joyful with friends in the backyard.

But there is a particular kind of joy that is experienced between parents and kids in playful, loving relationships. That kind of joy produces remarkable and long-lasting benefits for your child *and* for you.

When a child feels cared for, and knows that someone has concern for their well-being, they can tolerate the bumps and scrapes of daily life.

When we experience joy together with others in a loving connection, it triggers a biological, neurological response in both our bodies. The brain's reward system responds to loving care. Hormones, such as oxytocin, are released that bring feelings of safety, calm, and happiness. Natural opioids in the brain relieve feelings of pain and anxiety. This is why a mother's kiss makes a child's scraped knee hurt less.

In the short term, joy eases stress for you and your child and supports cooperative behavior. Over time, you will find it easier to relax and enjoy each other's company more often. When you need to teach or discipline, you won't have to work so hard to be heard.

In the long term, this joyful relationship supports healthy brain development and helps to build resilience. You're also creating a relationship roadmap because positive experiences with you prepare your child to experience healthy relationships in years to come.

Why Read This Book?

My to-do list is endless, and it already takes all my energy to make it through the day. I've got a lot of parenting books already. Unless this one can get my kid into college someday, I don't have time.

Does this sound like you?

As parents ourselves, we understand. We have struggled with competing interests: being the best mom or dad we can be, versus simply making it through the day without losing our—well, you know.

Way more often than not, just making it through each day wins.

But here is why you should read this book:

- It takes just seconds to do the things we describe.
- No extra time is required in your day. You can do these things in the course of your typical day.
- It actually could help your kid get into college. Really. This book will help your child thrive in whatever direction they choose. The activities in this book will wire your child's brain for resilience in all areas: in learning, taking on challenges, creating healthy relationships, and coping with the hard knocks of life.

The science of brain development is clear: Positive, playful interactions have incredible benefits for the growing child. And you, the parent, benefit as well.

These Joyful Together activities are organized to fit into the most hectic family life. Most activities do not require any materials. All are easy to do. The goal is simply to promote positive interactions between you and your children. We believe that play and care lead to joy, joy leads to emotional connection, connection builds resilience, and resilience leads to more successful emotional, social, and cognitive development.

Joyful Together Activities

The best and easiest way for parents to spark joyful connections with their kids is to do simple, fun, playful activities together. We call them Joyful Together activities. You can use one of these activities to transform an otherwise ordinary, everyday moment into a relationship-building moment—just with several seconds of eye contact, touch, or laughter.

A Joyful Together activity is:

- For two people at a time (although everyone around you can enjoy them)
- Fun
- Easy to do
- Flexible
- Free
- Non-competitive
- Short and sweet. A few seconds is enough (but you can take longer if you like).

How does a Joyful Together activity work? What does it look like, sound like? To give you an idea, here are a few examples of the many ways we've seen parents use Joyful Together activities with their kids:

Example 1: How Tall Am I?

It's time for bed, and 5-year-old Aidan is dawdling. His mom wants to get him on track.

"Let's see how many toothbrushes tall you are," she says, taking his purple toothbrush off the sink. She places it along Aidan's side, sliding it up and counting one toothbrush-length at a time. "One, two, three . . . Wow—you're eight-and-a-half toothbrushes tall! After you brush, let's see how many pillows tall you are."

Example 2: Hot Cocoa

Polly, a toddler, is having a bad day. Everything leads to a tantrum. When her mom simply tries to put in a hair clip, Polly screams.

This time, Mom squeezes her in a warm, tight hug, and says, "You are like a mug of hot cocoa—but too hot to drink! Can I blow on you to cool you down?"

"No!" Polly squeals, but she lets Mom keep holding her.

"You smell so yummy. Mmmm!" Mom sniffs Polly's hair. "I'm going to add whipped cream so you smell even yummier." She swirls Polly's hair just a little.

"No," Polly says again, but she starts to giggle. "Add marshmallows!" she says.

Mom pretends to plop marshmallows on Polly's head. "Plop, plop, plop!" And puts in the hair clip while she's at it.

Example 3: Eye Hugs

Jason hurries aboard the school bus, jostling with friends. He hates saying goodbye to his dad. He doesn't want his friends to think he's a baby. Taking his seat, he looks out the bus window and sees his dad standing on the sidewalk with the other parents. His dad looks straight back at him. They lock eyes, lift their eyebrows, and give each other a small smile. Both of them know this secret: an Eye Hug has just been shared. It's a code Jason and his dad use with each other to say, "See you later. Love you!"

Do these examples seem rather simple and maybe a little silly? Yes! Were they planned ahead? Not really. It might take a little practice to pull off a good "Hot Cocoa" in the middle of a tantrum, or to execute a long-distance "Eye Hug"—but only a little.

Later in the book we have a chapter with "recipes" for dozens of

Joyful Together activities just like these. The instructions are all super simple. Each activity can take a few seconds or a few minutes. You'll try a few, find some you like, and be able to call on your favorites whenever and wherever you need them.

A skeptical therapist

Confession time: I was a skeptic.

The concept of Joyful Together was created by the chief clinical officer of the agency where I worked as a therapist with mostly low-income families who had experienced ongoing trauma and hardship. I was assigned to a team that was told to develop strategies for improving relationships and resilience between parents and kids. We brainstormed for several weeks and came up with more than one hundred activity ideas.

It just seemed too easy.

Then I was tasked with the next step: Try out the games with families and capture the results on video.

My expectations were low. The families I worked with were often coping with serious problems, such as poverty, traumatic experiences, and extreme stress, and the strategies just seemed . . . *fun*. How could they possibly make an impact?

Reluctantly, I brought a list of Joyful Together activities and my video skills to the home of 5-year-old Leon (not his real name) and his family.

They lived in a high-crime neighborhood near downtown Cleveland. They had experienced several horrific years in Leon's short life, marked by violence and loss. Leon's mother accepted therapy for her child, but was too overwhelmed by her own grief to participate. She seemed indifferent to me, to the goals of our work together, and, often, to Leon. I was skeptical that Leon's mother would even participate in the activities because she had rarely taken part in our sessions before.

Imagine my surprise as I watched this family transform.

We started with an activity called "I Love You Echoes," with Leon and his mother squeaking, growling, whispering, and yelling, "I love you!" back and forth across the kitchen table to each other. Soon they were next to each other, touching and hugging. Then they decided to play the game as they danced, copying each other's moves as they continued to say "I love you" in funny voices.

This family was doing it! Not only did they enjoy the activity, they created their own version! And they didn't stop there. We spent over an hour trying new Joyful Together activities.

I'll never forget watching the family play "Let's Take a Trip," pretending to go to the barber shop and beauty salon. At one point, tough little Leon was gently "washing" his mother's hair; her eyes were closed as she leaned her head back in a state of bliss.

These simple, fun activities enabled Leon and his mother to connect and show love to each other in a way that a year of therapy hadn't been able to. The success of each activity led mother and child to want to try more activities. The loop of fun, laughter, and care led to more fun, laughter, and care.

This was my first glimpse at the power of Joyful Together.

Joy

We already introduced the concept of joy. But because it's so essential, we want to tell you a little more about it. Remember, we're talking about a specific kind of joy here: The neurophysiological kind. The brain and body working together kind. That kind makes a huge difference to your child.

That kind of joy actually has a very simple recipe. Just two ingredients: play and care.

We're talking about particular kinds of *play* and *care* here. Those two terms were given specific meaning by the pioneering neuroscientist and psychobiologist Jaak Panksepp. He used them to describe two positive *affective* (or emotional) processes in the human brain. These unconscious processes guide us throughout our lives. Here's what they mean to you and your child . . .

Play

You know your kids like to play.

Did you know they really *need* to play, too?

Biologically, children are hard-wired to play. It's crucial to all aspects of healthy development: physical, cognitive, emotional, interpersonal, and moral. Evidence is mounting that play and movement are critical to analytical thinking and academic performance, too.

To deliver these benefits, play should be unstructured, child-motivated, and creative, so that children can get "lost" in their thoughts.

When they can create their own worlds, with their own rules, they gain a sense of mastery because they are in charge. Play is the practice ground for developing executive function skills, such as planning ahead, regulating energy, and adapting to changing circumstances.

Kids need a variety of opportunities for play:

Indoor and outdoor.

Calm and active.

Messy.

Loud.

Sometimes even rough.

In fact, just like all other mammals, kids need rough-and-tumble play. Your child really is behaving like a wild animal! Play-fighting, tackling, and other "wild" behavior serves a purpose: It helps kids practice motor, social, and relationship skills. It teaches them how to initiate and maintain interactions with others. Play also enhances empathic capacities.

Play is not frivolous. It is as fundamental to healthy human development as it is fun.

Care

Care, in this context, is our natural tendency to be concerned about the welfare of others, especially the young. (It's the care urge that makes us want to cuddle baby animals.) Our kids rely on us for everything: safety, food, shelter, and emotional support. They also share the natural attraction we all have to one another, a need for connection.

When we feel more connected, we feel more cooperative, too. This is true for all of us, adults and children. When we feel loved, we relax. We are able to listen and learn. We feel safe with others, and we trust that the world is a happy place.

Loving care creates secure attachment. It feels like magnets attracting.

Play + care = joy

When your child engages with you in playful activity while experiencing a sense of caring connection, that's when joy happens. That's when those hormones and brain chemicals are released that help reduce stress and build positive energy. You laugh and smile together, and you want to keep laughing and smiling together. When you experience some joy, you want more joy. You want to keep being happy together.

That's why Joyful Together activities are not "just" fun. They have real and lasting physical and emotional benefits for you and your child.

Joy Language

"As a child, I remember being at my grandparents' house in the summertime, helping in the garden. The tomato plants were as tall as I was because I was so small. My grandfather let me run through the garden and didn't tell me to be careful—he knew that I would be OK because he had taught me how to care for the plants. Even today, when I smell fresh garden tomatoes, I feel calm and comforted, as if my grandfather were still with me."

Linda's face lit up as she told this story. Now a mother of two, Linda often finds herself in the garden with her children. It's where she feels most connected and calm and happy with her kids. She had not realized it, but gardening together with family was her "joy language."

We all have a joy language (often more than one), although we may not always recognize it. Your joy language is the way that you have fun with your child. It is anything that you do that brings a shared experience of joyful connection.

Remember, joy changes your brain as neurochemicals are released that positively affect your body, mood, and behavior. It comes from the experience of co-regulation in the context of a relationship that provides trust, understanding, love, and care. And when we experience joy with someone we love, we want more of it because the connection feels so good.

Your joy language is how you make that connection. It is often rooted in your earliest experiences.

For Linda, her early experiences of gardening with her grandfather led her to create similar experiences with her children. She and her children are drawn to the outdoors and to working together on projects, just like Linda and her grandfather had been years earlier.

Everyone experiences joy differently

For some people, joy is exuberant and active. For others, it is quiet. There are as many ways to experience joy as there are people in the world.

Linda and her family find joy in being together outdoors. Gardening and walking in the woods are activities that bring them together emotionally. At those times, they are most likely to relax and to laugh. After a stressful week, Linda plans outdoor time with her kids. She knows that the following week will go more smoothly, and that she and her kids feel calmer after being together in this way.

Holli's joy language is rough-and-tumble. She loves to wrestle and run with her kids.

Melissa's joy language is artistic. She loves to paint, draw, and create with her kids.

John's joy language is athletic. After a few minutes in the yard throwing a ball, he and his kids feel relaxed and connected.

Joy is not about "Disneyland moments"—elaborate events or big occasions. Joy is in the everyday moments of play, laughter, and connection. That's where your joy language is, too.

There are many ways to experience joy and play.

Joy can be:

- Active—running, dancing, climbing
- Quiet—art, building with blocks/Legos
- Messy—mud pies, finger painting
- Rough-and-tumble—wrestling, play fighting
- Athletic—playing catch
- Nurturing—dolls, playing house

You can even sing, hug, smile, or simply look into someone else's eyes and feel joy and connection.

What matters is that you and your child experience these feelings together—being joyful together!

Finding your joy language

To find your joy language, look to your past. Joy we experienced as children still feels like joy to us now, as adults.

Holli, whose joy language is roughhousing with her kids, realized that her fondest childhood memories involved similar play with her father.

Linda's joy language began with sharing her grandfather's garden.

Our joy language is woven into the relationship map that we developed with our earliest caregivers. We seek that which we recognize from our past. We find comfort in experiences that feel familiar.

Reflect on your childhood

Recall a time in your childhood when you experienced joy with a caregiver—a parent, grandparent, teacher, coach, or religious leader, for example.

What springs to mind?

Is there a moment when you felt completely safe and happy?

Was there an adult in your life who made you feel unconditionally loved?

Was there an adult who you loved to be around because they were fun and made you feel good?

When you remember yourself playing as a child, who were you with? What were you doing? Did you ever play with your parents? If so, what did you like? If you didn't play with your parents, how did that make you feel? Reflecting on your past can help you get in touch with what your child feels like now.

Doing this exercise might also help you remember important relationships you had as a child, and how joy can be experienced in different contexts, such as school or at summer camp. These memories might inspire you to create similar experiences with your own child.

In doing this exercise, if you feel you lacked some things in your own childhood, that's OK. Consider how you might give your child the emotional experiences that you wish you had had.

A note about painful memories

For some people, it is painful to remember childhood. They might have experienced hardship or abuse. If you are one of those people, here's the good news: It can be different for your own children! The fact that you are reading this book means that you are committed to your relationships with your children. Now, as you reflect on your childhood, instead imagine the caregiver you wish you had had. Use your not-so-good experience as motivation for creating a better experience for your own child.

Sorry, playing with kids just isn't my thing

I'm not really the type to play with my kid. I don't get on the floor or cluck like a chicken. I don't pretend that I can blow kisses and wave them around with an invisible wand.

Does this sound like you?

Maybe when you were growing up, your parents sent you off to play on your own. It wasn't right or wrong—it was just what people did.

Maybe you believe it's not good to play with kids—your child might become too relaxed around authority figures and wind up getting into trouble.

Maybe you think play is for children to experience with other children. (It *is* great to see them laugh and run together with other kids while also learning some social skills, like sharing things. And if we're honest, we're also relieved at times just to get them out of our hair.)

But if you don't enjoy playing with your kids, can you even use Joyful Together?

Yes.

Good news: In Joyful Together, *play* really means *anything you do with your child that brings a smile or a moment of happiness to each of you.*

Even when you simply bring a playful spirit to putting your toddler's shoes on, that experience changes from merely a chore to an opportunity for connection. ("Your shoes are on—elbow kiss!")

Joyful Together is about using small moments in the course of a typical day to tune in to each other.

You don't have to sit on the floor pretending to like playing house while your mind actually scrolls through your to-do list.

Joyful activity might look as simple as this:

- doing your "secret handshake" at school drop off;
- waking your child up with his special kiss;
- starting dinner with a round of Wishes for the World.

Joyful activity might take 5 seconds. But if you are both happy, and you are both having fun, it might go on for 30 minutes.

Play is whatever you make it. You decide—you and your child.

What if you're not the "fun" parent?

John did not think of himself as a "fun dad." He loved his kids, and mostly enjoyed being around them, but he had never felt comfortable roughhousing or being silly. The idea of playing with his kids made him tense up. Here's how John was able to use Joyful Together to support positive behavior in his family in ways that felt comfortable for him.

At dinnertime, John's three kids hated sitting still around the table. They bounced around like pinballs, getting up from their chairs, running around the kitchen, never stopping to eat, talk, or be quiet.

John tried different things: yelling, ignoring the behavior, giving warnings about consequences to come. Sometimes those things worked. But mealtimes were the most calm and pleasant when John began doing Joyful Together activities.

He started with the "Mirror Game" with one child, who caught on quickly to the game of making a small change to his expression and his father copying it.

When the other kids noticed, they settled down. They wanted to try the game, too.

Dinner took on a different energy level. Everyone was more settled. When the kids started to get antsy again, John switched to a different game: "Pass It On!" He would touch a child's arm or make a funny sound and say, "Pass it on!" until it reached everyone in the family.

When John felt like it, he added new games to the dinner routine.

He learned that he didn't have to be energetic and loud—a style that just didn't fit his personality. He was able to find and use activities that felt comfortable to him. In doing it his way, he was authentic in his style of playing—and the kids were drawn to it.

Using Joyful Together
With Your Child

OK, you're still with us. You've heard about the magic of joy. You've tapped into your special memories of joy. Now, you're willing to give Joyful Together a try. How do you start?

It's simple. Really.

You don't need special skills or training to use Joyful Together in your family. You just need to be curious. Will this make my kid laugh? Will this make us feel better together?

Almost anything goes! If you are laughing together, that's joy. If your moods improve, that's joy. If a power struggle ends with a hug instead of tears—that's joy!

Joyful Together activities are simple. Many of them have been around forever. You may already do some of them with your kids.

The difference is the intent: With Joyful Together you are intentionally seeking connection with your child with the goal of improving your relationship.

You may feel awkward at first. That's OK! The more you practice, the easier it gets.

Here are some tips for getting started.

Start with the fun part: Pick a few Joyful Together activities to try together

Flip to the back of the book where the Joyful Activities are collected. Read through them. Imagine yourself doing these activities with your child. Put a checkmark next to a few that you think you might want to try.

Joyful Together activities are most effective one-on-one. Think through the activities with each of your kids in mind. Something that works with one kid might flop with another.

Also consider your home environment and routine. Imagine when and where you will do each activity. Consider these factors:

- What time of day works best for you and each child?
- What is each child's joy language?
- What Joyful Together activities might match your child's joy language and your own joy language?
- What opportunities can you find to give your full attention to your child, even if only briefly?

Prepare to be fully present

Children know when we are paying attention to them and when we are not. Prepare to bring your full attention to your Joyful Together interactions with your children. Quiet your thoughts and your body. Breathe. Be aware of your intentions (Children also know when we have an ulterior motive). Take several seconds to focus only on what is happening in the moment.

This is difficult to do, especially in the hustle and bustle of a busy day. But do your best. Know that it gets easier as you practice. Understand that you will be better at it some days than others.

Notice the tiny shifts that occur when you successfully connect with your child, especially when you're in a challenging phase of his development (like the terrible twos or threes). Does your breathing get easier? Does a smile spring to your face? Do your shoulders relax?

Notice what happens to your child. How does his behavior, body, or mood change?

Celebrate the moments of connection, and reflect on them later. Remember that these moments last well beyond that day. Your child will store that memory, and, like money in the bank, will draw on that memory when times are tough.

The more joy you experience together, the greater the likelihood that there will be joy in the future.

Make a plan

As you experiment with the activities, it helps to have a simple plan. Your chances of success are better if you think ahead. Eventually, you'll do it without even thinking. But at first . . .

- Start small: Pick a few activities and add more as you become comfortable.
- Make a cheat sheet: Write out the instructions so you remember what to do.
- Pick a time of day, such as wake-up time, school drop-off, or dinnertime.
- Prepare to scrap the plan. Kids bring their own moods and needs to each moment and might not always be receptive to an activity. That's OK! Try again later.
- Note the challenges and use that information as you plan for future activities.

Use the activities you selected

The goal is to experience joy in the moment. There is no right or wrong way to make this happen, but here are some helpful tips:

- Start by following the outline provided for each activity, but know that it's OK to make your own changes at any time. Take cues from your child and adjust accordingly.
- Be curious: *Let's try this and see what happens.*
- Follow your instincts. Do what feels fun or right in the moment.

- Lead your child by *doing*, rather than *telling*.
- Avoid competition. An activity with winners and losers is not conducive to joy. Turn competitive energy into cooperation by focusing on connection, not winning.
- Allow an activity to reach a natural conclusion, whether that takes five seconds or five minutes. Notice your child's cues: laughing and smiling, or inattentive, crying, defiant, etc.
- Try as many activities as you can—even ones that seem boring or ridiculous. You never know how your child will respond!
- Jot down a list of your favorite activities. Keep adding to it.
- Maintain your own sense of joy and optimism. Your kids will take their cues from you.

Keep track of your success

Make it a habit to use Joyful Together throughout the day, every day. Put it on your calendar. Try new games. Make notes about what your kid liked and didn't like. Challenge yourself to make up your own activities.

At the same time, note the changes in yourself and your child. Are you having fewer power struggles? Is bedtime any easier?

Keeping track of your successes will keep you accountable. It will deepen your commitment to using Joyful Together to improve your relationship with your child.

Troubleshooting

You might encounter a few challenges, especially when you first start using Joyful Together activities. Here are some of them, and what to do about them.

You just can't connect with your child. (You and your child speak different joy languages.)

- Experiment with different games and activities.
- Let your child take the lead.
- Join your child in an activity she enjoys.
- Start small: moments of eye contact, a smile, a gentle touch.
- Take it slowly.
- Don't give up!

Reflect: What attitude, tone, and body language are you modeling? Are you behaving in a way that invites your child toward you?

Your child's behavior gets worse

When kids feel threatened or overwhelmed, they act out. If Joyful Together activities seem to be making things worse, pause and regroup.

Notice:

- What signals is your child giving about her feelings or needs?
- What makes this child feel good?
- When is this child most likely to be happy?

Reflect:

- What thoughts do you have about your child as you interact with him?
- If you have negative thoughts about your child, do you have a friend, family member, or other support person who can help you manage these feelings?
- Are you approaching your child with a mindset or expectation that leaves little room for change? ("She never listens!")
- Are you choosing activities that are conducive to the setting and

mood? For example, bedtime is not the time for Simon Says: Balance!

Doing Joyful Together activities feels awkward

Playing and being silly with kids can make adults feel vulnerable. We understand! Start slowly. Try different activities. Don't give up! The more you practice, the easier the activities become.

Reflect on your joy language. Use your memories of childhood to guide you toward joyful connections with your kids.

There's no time to do Joyful Together activities—or anything else!

The beautiful thing about Joyful Together is that it takes only a moment. The activities are designed to happen within the regular activities of the day.

Examples of families using Joyful Together are found throughout the book. Other examples are:

- Give your child a wizard kiss as he gets on the school bus.
- Touch elbows with your child after she ties her shoes.
- "Draw" a smiley face on your child's palm as you tuck her into bed.

There are bigger issues

Sometimes there are bigger issues that get in the way, like depression or anxiety in the parent or child, or other mental health issues. Your pediatrician is an excellent source of information and can help you distinguish typical childhood development from a more serious issue. For adults, your primary care physician can be a helpful starting place for seeking mental health care. If you suspect that you or your child are struggling with mental health challenges, Joyful Together will not be a cure. However, Joyful Together can be a useful supplement to professional care.

Why adults sometimes have to work at it

Not all parents love to play with their kids. That's perfectly normal. Some of it is actually biological. Adult brains function a little differently from kids' brains.

As adults, we make our lists and plans, and we get things done. We tend to be logical, with one thing leading to the next.

Children tend to be more in the moment—experiencing the world with all their senses. This means they are spontaneous—and primed for play. Your child's spontaneity, his here-and-now mindset, is what we capitalize on to create moments of joy.

Does this mean I'm supposed to be joyful all the time?

You don't have to be joyful all the time. That's impossible.

Relationships have stress. Days are full of chores and obligations, and just as we are hard-wired for relationships, we are also hard-wired to experience a variety of emotions.

Joyful Together is about finding opportunities for connection in spite of all the challenges of a normal day. It's about learning to define joy as our good feelings about being in this moment together, whatever this moment looks like.

Too tired for joy? You'll be surprised

"When I came home, the last thing I felt like I wanted to do was to play with my kids," says Holli, a therapist and mother of two.

Like so many of us, she would come home from a workday tired.

And she felt the pressure to keep going, to get to the evening routine: dinner, dishes, bedtime stories, and baths.

"Now, I stop to lie in the middle of the living room for five or ten minutes and let my kids dive-bomb or tickle."

Spending a few minutes doing Joyful Together activities when she comes home has made all the difference, she says.

"Sometimes, we do 'Steamroller.' I pretend to roll them down a hill, pushing on their shoulders and hips. I'll say, 'There's a big rock in the road! Let's roll, roll, roll!'

"It all takes no time at all, and there's no denying how much different my body feels—my energy level lifts."

Just do it

Getting out of the house every morning was a battle for the Martin family. Parents and kids screamed at each other, and the day always seemed to start on a bad note.

When everybody got home again at night, it was sometimes hard to forget the awful things that had been said.

Joan wanted to help her family turn things around.

She created a "Secret Handshake" with each of her kids—the last thing they would do before saying goodbye for the day.

Joan did not always feel like doing it.

Sometimes she felt irritated.

Often, she was already in work mode, focused on the pressures of the day to come.

But she did it anyway, and that one small shift—a simple, silly, special handshake with each of her children—created a sea change in the Martin family.

Before separating for the day, every person in the family felt loved.

What If It Doesn't Work the First Time?

Joyful Together might work in fits and starts, and that's perfectly OK. It can take a little experimentation to find the activities that are just right for you.

That was true for Juana and Thomas, who had two extremely active girls, ages 3 and 6. Although the parents were eager to try Joyful Together, their girls often didn't seem interested. And sometimes when they were engaged, the activities actually wound the girls up and made them wild and unruly, and then Juana and Thomas couldn't settle them back down.

They experimented with different activities at different times of day.

They learned that "Stop 'n' Go" worked like magic when they needed an "off" button—a way to calm down.

Juana and Thomas would say "Run, run, run . . . Stop!" Doing this several times in a row let the kids practice shifting from high energy to calm—without feeling like their parents were controlling them. The game respected their energy.

They discovered that playing "Dance Party" allowed the kids to be energetic, but also safe.

Best of all, they discovered that various hugging games helped the girls join together with their parents even if their energy was high or their mood was silly.

Here's how it looked for Juana and Thomas and their girls as they experimented:

Sometimes it doesn't work . . .

Attempt #1

It's bedtime, and Juana tries to play "My Way Superhighway" with her 3-year-old. She pretends that her finger is a race car and zooms around her daughter's arms and legs.

Her daughter shrieks and laughs; it's too tickle-y!

Juana tries to be more gentle and calm. She slows down, using her hand to zoom so the pressure is more firm on her daughter's body.

Too late. The little girl is bouncing on the bed, zooming her hands around her mother's body, wound up like a race car.

Sleep is delayed by half an hour.

Attempt #2

The family is trying to enjoy a meal together. The girls are getting noisy. The parents try the "Wishes for the World" game.

The girls wish for poopy pants—and laugh hysterically.

Dinner ends with everyone upset.

Attempt #3

Thomas and his daughters are walking around the block. He wants to try "Let's Take a Trip," and says to the girls with excitement, "Let's pretend we're going on a mission. We're going to explore the world together! Where should we go?"

His daughters ignore him. They run ahead.

Sometimes it does . . .

Success #1

It's bedtime for the 3-year-old, who would rather be downstairs with her sister. The little girl is wiggly and energetic. She lies down, pops up, then flops back down. She jumps onto her mother's lap, then crawls around to her back.

Juana says, "I wonder how a penguin kisses?"

Her little girl bounces on the bed as she says, "Like this!" And she pretends to kiss the air.

Her mother says, "How does a puppy kiss?"

Mother and daughter trade ideas for "Animal Kisses."

Juana lets her daughter jump a few more times, then scoops her into a "bear kiss," which involves a big, gentle hug and lots of kisses on the little girl's face.

Soon, they try a "kitty cat kiss," which involves cuddling together in a warm basket—the child's bed. Juana's daughter gets calmer as the pace of the game slows down.

It seems as though sleep is a possibility after all.

Success #2

The family is trying to enjoy a meal together. The girls are getting noisy.

"Here comes 'Finger Man'!" Thomas says, making his fingers run between the girls' plates. "Finger Man doesn't know what to eat first: the beans or the potatoes. Which should he choose?"

The girls laugh. They decide what Finger Man should eat. They take turns "being" Finger Man. Juana and Thomas consider mealtime a success.

Success #3

Thomas and his daughters are walking around the block. He wants to play "Let's Take a Trip," but his daughters are busy pushing each other and yelling at each other.

Thomas says, "Guys, listen! If we act fast, we can be the first astronauts on Pluto!"

The girls aren't sure what he's talking about, but they chase after him, eager to take part in the excitement.

What was the difference?

Why did Joyful Together work some of those times and not others? It's not just about what activities you choose or create. It's about the mood and energy each of you brings to the moment. It's about being sensitive to what your child needs and what you can handle.

Read your child's cues and body language. Check in with yourself.

When using Joyful Together activities, it's a dance between parent and child, with each partner equally important to its success. The positive feelings of one partner should never come at the expense of the other partner.

Joyful Together is not about guilt—it's not about what you "should do" to be a "good parent." It is about intentionally creating positive connections with your child, over and over again, because it feels good for both of you.

Not every activity will work for every parent and child. Pick the ones that seem the most accessible to you.

Try one.

Try it again.

Activities may feel awkward at first, but keep practicing. You will naturally get better at drawing your child into the activities as you become more aware of your child's subtle mood changes.

You'll notice which activities make you laugh, and which calm you down; which are helpful at bedtime, and which are best for the playground.

Your child will provide you with important information:

He will laugh harder at some activities than others.

She will ask for certain activities.

He will try certain activities with his siblings and friends.

Take note! These are the activities to keep handy in your mind, to be used over and over again. These are the ones that will probably turn into your family's own shorthand for "I love you."

The most important thing you will notice is that you and your child are having more moments of connection and fewer moments of conflict.

More About Why Joyful Together Works

Mirroring

Have you ever yawned after seeing someone else yawn? Of course. This happens all the time.

That behavior is caused by mirror neurons, parts of our brain that notice and feel what other people's brains are experiencing.

When your child falls down, he looks immediately at your face to see how he feels. His look asks, *Am I OK?* When we recognize that our child is not hurt, in a split second of unconscious thought, we say, "You're OK."

Our calm handling of the situation helps the child feel calm, too.

Our mirror neurons allow us to guess at what our babies need when they are too little to tell us with words. Our awareness of how uncomfortable it feels to be hungry gives us a sense of urgency when we think our baby is hungry. In a sense, we feel the baby's hunger, too.

Similarly, our kids' mirror neurons allow them to absorb our emotions. When we are stressed, our kids can tell. When we are at ease, our kids feel at ease. Mirror neurons help our kids make sense of the world.

Joyful Together activities take advantage of this built-in process. They work with our natural desire to tune into our child's emotional world, and our child's natural desire to tune into ours.

A Joyful Together activity is like a game of catch with your child:

You toss her an elbow kiss, and she tosses it back. You and your child are always "tossing" your emotions back and forth, whether you realize it or not.

In Joyful Together, you practice this with the activities, laughing and sharing attention in a playful mood. You and your child get better and better at reading each other's signals. Together, you build an investment in your relationship, which can be drawn upon in the difficult moments. The more positive moments you invest, the easier it is to return to connection when times are hard.

Even if it feels like you make the same mistakes over and over with your kids—even if you feel like you're angry or upset more than you want to be—change is possible.

The rough spots won't disappear. There will always be conflicts between parents and kids. But you can make sure that there are good times, too. You can use your awareness of mirror neurons to intentionally create and find connections with your kids.

Co-regulation

Another back-and-forth process humans share is a bit like mirroring but more complex and more powerful. It's called *co-regulation*. This is the superpower that can actually change your child's mood—and your own.

Our kids have big feelings, just like we do, and sometimes they need help handling them. When you comfort your child when she's sad, mad, or scared, she builds the ability to handle these feelings herself.

Newborn babies illustrate the concept of co-regulation well: When we pick up a newborn, our bodies naturally soften and sway; we understand that our bodies impact the baby's comfort. If the baby starts fussing, we stand up and bounce; when the baby calms down, we move more slowly.

Adults seek co-regulation, too. Think of a time when you received bad news. You didn't get the promotion you'd been working toward for months, or a trip you were looking forward to got cancelled. Did you tell someone close to you about your disappointment? Ask yourself: *Why did I reach out to that person?* Maybe your conversation focused on practical things—future career plans, other trips, but did you feel better afterward? Did you feel reassured? You just went through a process of co-regulation.

Co-regulation is the influence people have on each other in relationships.

When your child is very young, you are largely responsible for his comfort. As he grows, he takes on more and more responsibility for it. As you help him through life's challenges, he learns about himself and others.

Co-regulation can come in the form of a hug, verbal reassurance ("You can handle this"), or a smile. Anything that sends a message of care moves your child toward co-regulation. In these moments of providing comfort, you are helping your child feel safe and calm.

This back-and-forth process helps your child make sense of her feelings. The ability to regulate her own emotions is what enables your child to cope with life's challenges.

Help, this kid is out of control!

When our kids misbehave, it's often because they feel disconnected from us, not because they just feel like breaking the rules.

Do you notice that as soon as you start talking on the phone, your child suddenly has an important question for you or really wants you to pick her up? She knows that your attention is on the phone and away from her; she feels disconnected, and that feels uncomfortable. If this happens frequently, the uncomfortable feelings inside your child get bigger and bigger.

When you notice that your child is struggling to listen or is testing your rules, look for opportunities to connect with her.

This doesn't mean that you ignore misbehavior; parents

make the rules, and rules must be followed. But recognize that misbehavior means that your child needs your help. By breaking the rules, your child is getting your attention and creating connection—just not in the way you'd like.

Resilience

Life brings challenges, and your child will experience many bumps and bruises—physically and emotionally. But the care of a loving adult and co-regulation enable your child to recover from each one. And over time, she learns to support herself.

This coping ability is called resilience.

Joyful Together activities are designed to help build long-term resilience in your child. They use the co-regulatory process of back-and-forth sharing of emotions. The more you and your child use these activities, the better you get at reading each other's signals. You become more tuned in to your child's moods and needs. You also become more aware of how your child tunes in to your moods.

The more you use these activities, the better you and your child become at handling all your emotions. The positive connections you build with your child create a foundation that can withstand the challenges of day-to-day life.

When he doesn't make the soccer team, gets a bad grade, or the friend he trusted the most doesn't come through, he can handle it better.

In the long term, using Joyful Together you set your child up for strong, healthy relationships. Your child also learns to be resilient and to manage stress in a healthy way.

Children who can do this have a significant advantage. They learn better. They cope better. They bounce back.

They thrive.

It's Never Too Late— or Too Early—to Use Joyful Together

Joyful Together activities can be adapted to work with any age, from before a child is born through the grandparent stage. It is never too early—or too late—for joy.

As Joyful Together was being developed, Georgie, a therapist, tested the activities on her teenaged boys.

"Obviously not all of the activities were appropriate, but I was able to find about five different ones that worked on some level. Often, it felt one-sided; I would pretend to drop-kick a kiss to my son across the living room, or do 'Brain Power' as I sent them off to school. They would roll their eyes, but I knew that in that moment *they* knew how important they were to me."

Joyful Together concepts will enhance any relationship, regardless of age.

It's not too late

Sometimes it feels like all we do as parents is screw up. We compare ourselves to others and come up short. We read articles and books about parenting and feel overwhelmed.

Sometimes, it feels like it's too late—even if our child is only 3 years old!

This parenting book is different. We believe that it is never too late to improve your relationship with your child.

In every interaction, we have a tiny opportunity to work toward the relationship that we want to have. Sure, our kids will still have bad moods, difficult experiences, and the developmental need to oppose us. We will still have bad moods, too, and we will still get tired. We will probably still lose patience with our kids more often than we'd like. Relationships sometimes get off course. Parents and children get in patterns of conflict, when everything feels like a battle and being together at all is difficult.

At times like that, it's hard to imagine wanting to play together because everyone is holding on to hurt feelings and anger. Everyone is afraid that getting too close will spark another fight.

Joyful Together offers a way out.

It's easier to start small.

Teach your child what an "Eye Hug" is and give him Eye Hugs all day long. Even if you don't totally feel like it. Even if he doesn't acknowledge you. Even if he doesn't even know that you're doing it!

Of course, connection takes two. You need to get your child on board. How do you get a surly, grumpy child to connect? Slowly. Respectfully.

Notice opportunities for connection. Before you head out the door in the morning, connect. When you say goodnight, connect.

Tiny shifts in your attitude can create tiny shifts in your child's. Slowly, slowly, the changes become noticeable, bringing you and your child together again.

You can find new beginnings

Brittany, a therapist, has two daughters. In her second pregnancy, she needed weeks of bed rest, which included time in the hospital. Her older daughter was 2½ years old at the time. She was told, repeatedly, over three months, that her mother was "sick" and that was why she was away. When the family was finally all reunited, Brittany noticed that her daughter was acting up.

"She wasn't listening to me. I wanted her to be respectful and to listen, but she would look me dead in the face and refuse to do the things I asked."

Brittany says that as a mother, she needed to give herself permission to play. But things began to shift when she brought games into the mix.

"We started with a 'clean up song,' and I noticed that she was not only more cooperative, but I was less frustrated, too. It felt good."

Brittany says connecting joyfully worked hand-in-hand with all the other responsibilities of raising a child, such as instilling good values.

She and her children often invent and re-invent the activities. Even the same activities can look very different in different families.

Her daughters would play "Food Train" and pretend the fork or spoon was a train moving among the dinosaurs at Jurassic Park. Or they would eat their vegetables off the plates like a dinosaur.

They do "Thumb Kisses" and "Elbow Kisses" at church. When she dropped the children off at daycare, they would also do "Wizard Kisses"—waving their hands to direct and send kisses to one another through the air. This made the drop-offs much easier.

Joy during pregnancy

There are countless products on the market to boost your baby's intelligence (remember Baby Mozart?). But the best way to maximize your baby's potential is free: by enhancing the quality of the relationship you share with her.

Building that relationship starts in the womb. Your baby's senses are active in utero. As your body changes day to day, you are likely to have a heightened awareness of your own sensations and moods.

Your sensations and moods are intertwined with your baby's development and the experience of your pregnancy. Your relationship with your baby started on the day that you learned you were pregnant.

Enhance this relationship by asking yourself: How do I want to show up for my child? What qualities of my personality do I want to share with my baby? In what ways do I hope that my baby's childhood is similar to my own? Or different?

These questions can be a starting point for using Joyful Together during pregnancy. While you can't play games with your unborn baby, you can start connecting with him joyfully.

How to connect with your baby, joyfully

Breathe with your baby. Take a moment during the day to just sit with your baby and breathe.

Measure your belly. Use a tape measure to track the changes in your body as the weeks progress.

Play music and sing songs to your baby. Babies can hear sounds in the womb. Start teaching your baby your favorite songs.

Dance, exercise, and move your body.

As you do these activities, bring your attention to your baby. Know that you are investing in your relationship.

Challenges in pregnancy

Not every pregnancy is welcome or easy. Even if you are experiencing significant difficulties, small shifts can bring significant results. Start by acknowledging the hurdles (morning sickness, financial strain, family stress, or other things). Allow yourself to feel a range of emotions.

Know, also, that authentic joy is possible, even during the challenges.

Joyful Together is about authentic connection. The first step toward a healthy, authentic connection with your child is giving yourself permission to feel the hard stuff.

Without pushing the hard parts away, allow yourself to have feelings about your baby, too. You may find that you are able to make a distinction between the life challenges you face and your baby.

You may find that it is possible to make room for joy.

Joy with tweens

Yes, there are days when "joy" and "tween" might not sound like they go in the same sentence. This is a tender time of change and transition featuring emotional outbursts, eye rolls, slammed doors, quiet pouting, or perhaps some moody moping.

But even if you are just learning about Joyful Together at this stage, the concepts can benefit you both—helping you connect now and in years to come.

Mary, who has an 11-year-old son, Leroy, recounts her unique experience with Joyful Together . . .

My kid is on screens 24-7; it's all he does. I can't seem to get his eyes unglued from all his devices.

Sometimes I feel like I'm failing because I don't know how to make joy with him look very big or gregarious. I have trouble getting his attention.

And then there's guilt because of my own preoccupation with screens. I spend hours each day working and often not giving him the attention he needs. Instead, my nose is buried in emails.

I've come to understand something, though: There is no "perfect," and joy doesn't have to look a certain way.

Leroy isn't like the younger kids who romp around pretending to be at the zoo or on a treasure hunt.

I've learned from Joyful Together that I feel better about my parenting when I respect his timing and also when I respect the time I need for my work as well. For us, joy can be a squeeze of a hand or a light touch as we pass.

I've also come to invite connection later on, with more planning. We'll set it up, like an appointment. It can be a walk together with the dogs. Or some time in the kitchen together as I teach Leroy how to make cookies or French toast. It could even be joining him in playing a video game.

For us, this is what Joyful Together looks like.

Also, as I started doing these things with Leroy, something interesting happened. He began to give me more spontaneous hugs. He also started being more cooperative when I told him I needed to work and made plans to regroup later.

One morning, as he hugged me, he began to tap a drumbeat on my back with his hands. I started copying his beats on his back as we played "Pat a Beat."

Another time, I started with "I Love You Echoes," trading "I love yous" with him. I started saying it in other languages, "*Te amo*" and "*Eneh bee-hibuck*," until he said, "Mommy, I 'vuhl' you! That's pig latin!" We both burst out laughing. At that moment, I felt joy.

It's Time for a Joyful Together Activity When ...

We've gathered dozens and dozens of Joyful Together activities for you to try with your child. How do you know where to begin? Well, you almost can't go wrong, but some activities do seem particularly good for certain occasions. Here are a few examples to get you started.

When your kid is wild and you want him to calm down . . .

Telling your kid to "Calm down!" seldom works. (When's the last time you felt calmer after someone said that to you?) Instead, meet her energy with your own—then make it a game to calm down together.

Give her an Earthquake Hug! Wrap her in a big hug and rock her world. Gradually bring your intensity down but keep hugging. This helps her shift to a lower gear.

Try Stop 'n' Go: Tell him to "Go, go, go!" to build up the excitement. Then, "Stop!" Play a couple rounds, gradually bringing down the energy level by using a quieter voice and slower pace to your words and movements.

When you're somewhere where you are expected to be quiet . . .

Don't say, "Be quiet"; model it. Make your own voice quiet. Slow your movements. Rather than inviting a power struggle by trying to control your child, invite him into connection with a Joyful Together activity.

Are you in church? Try Pat a Beat: Hold your child's hand and gently pat it with the rhythm of the church music.

Try Breathing Buddies: Use your breath to show your child how to slow his body. Put your hands on your belly and show your child how it moves out and in with your breath. Tell your child that church is time to breathe slowly and move slowly. Breathe quietly together.

When you're waiting in line . . .

Focus on your child, not on your phone, with a quick game together. It will make him feel connected to you—and he'll have much more patience for waiting in line. Try Word Mirror: Pretend you and your child are both mirrors, and describe what you see. "I see a nose just like mine. I see smiling lips . . ." Then it's his turn: "What do you see?"

When your kid is scared to get a shot . . .

When we feel scared it can feel like there's nothing we can control— life is just coming at us and we can't make it stop. Give your child a feeling of control by playing Role Reversal: She gets to be the adult and tell you what to do. "Okay Mommy, get in the car. You have to get a shot."

When your child is nervous about going to school

What would you like to hear if you were feeling nervous? Tell it to your child. Play Brain Power: "I'm filling your brain with . . . confidence! And some extra love to get you through the day!" Let him know that he can do it, and that you understand what he is going through.

When you're trying to think but your child won't leave you alone . . .

Kids know when we're trying to get space from them, and it usually backfires—they feel rejected and get clingy. So do the reverse. Play Breathing Buddies: Invite your child to sit next to you so you can both breathe together.

When your kids are fighting . . .

Maybe they need a change of pace: play Pass it On! or What's Missing?

To help them vent: play Wishes for the World ("I wish I didn't have a sister!").

Change the scenery: get outside and play Cloud Party.

Get some energy out: have a Dance Party.

Help everybody reconnect: play Heart Hide 'n' Seek.

When it's time for bed . . .

Bedtime can be hard for kids because it feels like a separation from their special adults. Make bedtime a connection time instead, so your child looks forward to a few special minutes with you each night. Try playing Burrito Baby as you tuck your child snugly in the blankets.

When your child is grumpy about waking up for school . . .

It might feel like we're saving time by hurrying kids through their morning routine, but often we end up with grumpy kids. Which can make us feel grumpy. Take one extra minute to play Beep Game as you wake up your child: "Beep" in different voices as you press gently to wake up his legs ("Beep!"), nose ("Beep!"), eyelashes ("Beep!"), and elbows ("Beep!"). Your child might still be grumpy, but you've started his day with a connection, not a command. Doesn't that sound like an easier way to start the day?

When you have to say goodbye . . .

Pick a special hug and kiss and make them "your own." Practice the different hugs and kisses ahead of time and see which ones are especially fun with your child. Use them at every goodbye, to create a meaningful ritual.

Joyful Together
Activities

Here are more than 100 Joyful Together activities organized into four sections by suggested age ranges:

- Prenatal
- Birth to age 6
- Ages 6 to 12
- All ages

These age groupings are pretty loose. (For example, notice that 6-year-olds fit into three of the four sections!) Feel free to look in any section for an activity idea that seems right for you and your child.

When you find an activity that works for you, circle it, highlight it, or draw a smiley face next to it so you'll be reminded to use it again.

Then, pick another one to try!

Once you've got the hang of Joyful Together activities, you might come up with ideas of your own, too. That's great! You can use the blank pages at the end of this section to write those down.

Prenatal Activities

Pregnancy is a time of great change. Your body, emotions, and energy level change from day to day, and sometimes from moment to moment. Your relationships are affected, and as you consider life with a baby, the future suddenly has many more unknowns.

It is normal and healthy to experience a range of emotions during pregnancy, from excitement to boredom to gloom. Joyful Activities will not make difficulties go away. However, purposefully building your connection to your baby with joy supports a positive mood and begins building your relationship with your baby before he or she is even born.

You will not always be in the mood for joy, and that is OK. Allow yourself to feel and accept all of your moods. Do not put pressure on yourself to think or feel a certain way. When you feel up to it, try a Joyful Together activity. You may find that the activities can help you flip your mood from negative to positive, or that using the activities keeps you feeling more hopeful and happy more of the time. Experiment with different activities, and see what works for you.

Physical, emotional, and hormonal changes during pregnancy may be overwhelming at times. Sometimes pregnancy is unwelcome, or the timing is unexpected. Sometimes pregnancy puts women in touch with their pasts in uncomfortable ways, due to their own difficult childhood or to experiences that they had as young children.

Please be sure to seek help if you feel overwhelmed by your circumstances or your feelings. Your doctor or nurse is an excellent resource for information or referrals to therapists or support groups in your area.

Our hope is that using Joyful Together activities during pregnancy will set a tone of love and connection, and, of course, joy, in your relationship with your child in the months and years ahead.

The activities in this section are intended for use during the second and third trimesters of pregnancy. They are organized into three sub-sections:

Past—Activities that help you connect to your baby by reflecting on your past experiences and relationships.

Present—Activities focused on where you are today: your growing baby, your growing belly, and your changing life during pregnancy.

Future—Activities focused on the days and years ahead: routines and traditions, goals, and dreams for you, your baby, and your family.

Past

These activities ask you to connect to your baby by reflecting on your past experiences and relationships. Remembering joyful times from your past will help you create similar experiences for your baby. If you had a difficult past, identify ways that you can give your baby a more positive experience.

My Baby

Use a journal to write your thoughts, or, if you're feeling artistic, sketch a picture. Who do you think your baby will look like? What do you think your baby's personality will be? Reflect on images you've seen of yourself as a baby, or on old photographs of your siblings or parents. Ask questions of people who knew you as a baby or child, and find out what kind of a sleeper you were, or what your favorite foods were. Preparing for your new baby might prompt you to reflect on your own infancy and childhood. Becoming a parent allows us to understand our own parents in a new light. Art and journaling provide creative outlets for exploring the past and for anticipating the future with our baby.

*Please remember that some activities may cause difficult feelings to arise. Seek support if feelings become overwhelming, or if they interfere with daily functioning.

Love-In

Think about a person in your life who made you feel safe and loved. Maybe it's a family member, or maybe it was a teacher or coach from long ago. What was it about that person that made you feel so good? Identify the qualities that were special to you, such as kindness, laughter, acceptance, warmth, or generosity. Try to remember specific times when you interacted with that person and bring to mind those qualities that you most appreciated. Now bring those feelings to your baby. How can you help your baby feel safe and loved in similar ways?

Aspiration

Think of a person who is a good to her kids, who treats them in a way that you'd like to copy. Think of that person as you learn to be a parent yourself. Even if you've never seen that person deal with all the tasks of motherhood, try to imagine what she would do or say. Who do you want to be like as a mother? You might pick a teacher who always made you feel calm and accepted, or a TV mom who always uses humor to deal with hard times. Motherhood can be challenging. Who inspires you when times are tough?

Golden Opportunity

Think of something you wanted to do or to learn when you were young, but didn't have the opportunity. Did you want to learn to play a sport? Did you want to play the piano? Give your child a golden opportunity that you always wanted.

If the activity costs money, start looking into community organizations that offer scholarships. Music schools, community sports teams/recreation centers, and public schools may have programs that are right for you.

Traditions

Think of a tradition that you would like to start. Maybe it's a tradition you remember as a child or something brand new. Birthdays, holidays, first day of summer, or some random day that only your family celebrates—have fun coming up with a special way to mark the day.

Examples of birthday traditions:
- make paper cut-outs of your child's age and place them around the house—there's a 2 on the floor, the cereal bowl, the bathroom mirror, and the couch!
- take a photo with the same stuffed animal every year
- sing the birthday song in a special way
- special birthday meal
- write a note to the birthday child to tell him what you're proud of

Examples of holiday traditions:
- make homemade decorations together
- get together with extended family
- take a family photograph

Examples of random traditions:
- eat Popsicles on the first day of summer
- write a special note to your child on the first day of school
- always give a special hug and kiss when you say goodbye

Present

These activities are all about today: your growing baby, your growing belly, and your changing life during pregnancy.

Kick Counting

How many kicks can you feel? Place your hands on your belly and wait, or gently rub and poke your baby to see if he or she will respond with a kick. Take turns with each other: You move/touch/rub and see if your baby will also move. See if your partner or child can make your baby kick. You might notice that your baby is very active sometimes and very quiet at others.

Name That Body Part!

See if you can figure out your baby's different parts and positions as you both move through the day. Elbow or foot, head or bottom, what part of your baby is making that bump on your belly?

Little Peanut

Create a nickname for your baby. Pookie, Pumpkin, Pickle . . . anything goes! Talk to your baby using the nickname; at 19 weeks of pregnancy, he or she can begin to hear sounds outside the womb. This is a great way to start to connect with your baby, even if you haven't decided on an official name yet (or if you aren't ready to share the baby's name with others).

Onesie Wishes

Use a plain, light-colored onesie and fabric markers to write affirmations or wishes for your child. Write messages of love, hope, and joy, or decorate with symbols like hearts or stars. Imagine your baby wearing the onesie one day soon.

Weekly Selfie

Document your changing body with a weekly selfie. Try using the same pose at the same time each week, or just try to get regular photos of your growing belly. Include your partner or your other children, and if it feels fun, pose in funny or special ways (your older child kissing your belly, or sharing his Popsicle with your belly). Make a sign stating how far along you are in your pregnancy ("I'm 12 weeks along today!") or stating some fact about how your pregnancy is going ("All I want to eat is watermelon!" or "My favorite time to kick my mom is at 3 a.m.!"). Have fun coming up with your own ideas. Don't get discouraged if you forget to do this regularly, or only do it once or twice. Your photos will be keepsakes of your pregnancy.

Ultra-Memories

Collect your ultrasound photos in one place, such as a notebook, journal, photo album, or baby book. Write down your thoughts about each one, or details about the baby's development. Did your baby wave to you during the ultrasound? Jot that down! Was your baby active or sleepy? Did you find out the gender? Record any little details that occur to you. One day your grown-up baby will love to see these notes and memories.

Pregnancy Journal

Create a special keepsake about your pregnancy in a notebook or journal. Keep your ultrasound photos here, as well as any other details from your pregnancy that move you. For example, record gifts or advice you've been given, note your cravings, or write your dreams for your child. Note how far along you are in your pregnancy and your baby's growth ("It's week 18 and I think I feel you moving around in there!"), or what is going on for you ("I'm really craving spicy food, especially hot sauce."). You might also include details about your life, such as where you live, things you do for fun, or people who you spend time with. The normal, everyday events of your pregnancy will be interesting when you're looking back on them in the months and years to come.

You will probably want to share this memory book with your child one day, so remember to record only positive thoughts and memories (Use a private journal to explore your doubts and discomforts).

Remember When

Record your developing baby's "firsts": the first time you heard the heartbeat or felt a kick. When did you learn your baby's gender? When did you decide on the baby's name? Also record the events in your life (graduation, first apartment, or other transitions/accomplishments).

Basketball Baby

Take regular photos of your growing belly with the same object (such as a basketball), and then continue to take these photos as your baby grows. The object provides a fun comparison as you morph to new sizes, and then becomes a fun way to measure how quickly your baby grows.

Other fun ideas:
- a stuffed animal
- a special blanket
- a baby t-shirt or outfit
- a book that you can't wait to read to your child
- a photograph of an important person from your life or someone whose values you hope to match (such as a relative who has passed away, or a historical figure)
- a toy you loved as a child, or one that you wished you had as a child
- an object to represent your nickname for your child (Peanut, Pumpkin)

Stretching with Baby

Move your body, stretch your muscles, take care of your baby's first home—you! Yoga is a great way to get some exercise while you're pregnant, and there are lots of online resources to help you get started. Make sure to check with your doctor before exercising, and always listen to your own body. (If it feels uncomfortable, slow down or stop.)

As your body grows, your ability to exercise changes. You'll also notice that your baby reacts to your movements differently as your pregnancy progresses. Imagine that your baby is your exercise partner, cheering on your healthy habits.

Boy-Girl Blues

Are you secretly (or not so secretly) hoping for your baby to be a girl (or a boy)? How will you feel if your baby is not the gender you hoped for? Think this through for yourself now, so that in the delivery room you don't get a shock.

Ideas for coping with disappointment if your baby is not the gender you hoped for:
- talk about your disappointment with your partner, or with a trusted friend or family member
- accept your feelings—it's OK to feel disappointed

- identify the source of your disappointment (possibly with a counselor)
- identify ways to love the baby you get: for example, to teach your son to be the kind of man you would like him to become, or to decide to embrace your feminine qualities so that you can love your daughter's femininity

*Be sure to talk with your healthcare provider (doctor or nurse) if your negative feelings become too much to manage

Build a Mom

Create a collage with words, pictures, and drawings that describe your idea of being a mother. Will you be more of a kitten or a bear? A cookie baker or a carrot maker? Think of the things you loved or wanted from your own mother as you were growing up, or things you saw other mothers doing that you liked. If you love singing, add a picture of a music note or a lyric you love. Get your creative juices flowing. Include your values, your hopes, and your dreams. Look back on your collage as your baby grows, to remind yourself of the wonderful life you want for him.

Lifelines

In game shows, when a contestant is stuck on a question, they call their lifeline for help. Who is your lifeline? Think of a person in your life whom you can call when times are hard. A friend, family member, or community support who listens or helps can be a lifesaver during long, lonely days.

Healthy Habits Reminders

Make a list for yourself of habits to make and steps to take for a healthy pregnancy. Decorate sticky notes and place them around the house to help you remember your goals.

Take your prenatal vitamin.

Schedule your next doctor appointment.

Take a walk.

Write positive messages to yourself

Eat fruits and veggies.

Drink water.

Pregnancy and Baby Researcher

Incredible things are going on inside of you as your baby develops. Become a researcher: Use the Web to find one interesting fact about your pregnancy each week. Read it out loud to your baby.

Confidence Booster

Take some for yourself with a new hairstyle, fresh makeup, or a manicure. Celebrate your body and treat it well. Take a photo of yourself. Send yourself some love and confidence during this time of change.

Ch-ch-ch-ch-changing

Your body is changing every day as your baby grows. Your nails and hair may grow faster, your breasts and belly swell. Your senses and appetite get stronger. Take note of each change. Write down the changes in a journal or baby book. Celebrate the changes as signs that your baby is growing stronger each day.

Indulge Yourself

Once a week, let yourself indulge in the foods you most desire. Invite your partner or a friend to join you. Pickles and ice cream, spicy foods, cereal with orange juice . . . What are you craving? If your diet is healthy on most days, it's OK to splurge sometimes.

Record your cravings in a journal. You and your child can look back together at the wacky things you enjoyed in your pregnancy (like an Oreo covered with salami).

Your Baby's World

Imagine what your baby is thinking or feeling right now. When your baby is active, maybe she is excited about something you ate. When she's calm, imagine her enjoying the music you're listening to or your conversation with a friend. Notice the changes in your baby's movements throughout the day, and have fun imagining feelings or thoughts to match the movements.

You might also try tuning in to your baby's movements when you're feeling stressed or upset. See if you can calm yourself by gently rubbing your stomach, or by taking slow breaths. During pregnancy, your body is your baby's world. Bringing awareness to your baby, your body, and your breath supports you in feeling better together.

Baby Food

Notice how your baby reacts to the different foods you eat. See what happens when you eat spices, sweets, or comfort foods. Pay attention to the connection between what you eat and your baby's response.

Old Wives' Tales

Old wives' tales are stories people used to tell about how the world works—not based on science, but on the wisdom of the older women in the family. Many old wives' tales exist about predicting the gender of an unborn baby. Have fun trying out some of these examples (and you can look up more online):

Sweet vs. salty cravings—if you crave sweets, you're having a girl; salty cravings mean a boy

Excessive morning sickness means you're having a girl.

If your partner is gaining weight during your pregnancy, you're having a girl.

Feeling moody means girl; mellow means it's a boy.

Carrying your baby high means it's a girl, and low means a boy.

Tie a ring on a string and hang it over your belly. If it swings around in a circle, it's a girl; swinging side to side means a boy.

It's All Good!

It's normal to worry that you're doing something wrong in your pregnancy. Be thoughtful about your choices each day and do your best to make your baby's health and your own a priority. Then relax—it's all good! Focus on the positives, such as things you're already doing to care for yourself. Instead of worrying, use that energy for a walk. Invest yourself in positive activities so you have less time to think about negatives. Take care of yourself and think: It's all good!

Baby Mapping

Feel the lumps and bumps in your pregnant belly and figure out what they are. Bottom or head? Elbow or foot? Try to imagine how your baby is curled up inside you. Make a map in your mind of your growing child.

Breathing Buddies

Use your breath to help promote a feeling of calm and connection to your baby: become Breathing Buddies! Starting at 27 weeks, your baby practices using his lungs, inhaling and exhaling amniotic fluid. Imagine you are breathing together, mindfully taking each breath as you picture your baby doing the same. Your baby will sense your heart rate slowing as you relax your body with slow breaths. He will feel the movements as you inhale and exhale. Practice being your baby's Breathing Buddy throughout the day. Not only will you feel less stress, but your baby will, too.

Dance Party!

Feel the beat, move your hands and feet! Not only can your baby feel your movement starting at 23 weeks, but dancing is an excellent way to change the mood from down in the dumps to ready to roll. When you dance, your heart pumps, your body shakes off the tension of the day, and you're primed for laughter and connection with your dance partner—your baby!

Did your favorite song just come on the radio? It's Dance Party time!

Are you feeling extra sleepy? It's Dance Party time!

Don't let the lack of a radio stop this party; imaginary music is just as fun to dance to!

Sportscaster

Your baby can hear sounds outside of the womb starting at about 19 weeks, so let her know what's going on in the world. In the same way that a sportscaster describes each play on the athletic field, you describe what you are doing throughout your day. Walking to the bus stop, describe what you see, hear and smell. Getting ready for work, tell your baby what you have planned for the day, describe your outfit, and talk about the steps you're taking to get ready. This can feel silly at first, like you're talking to yourself, but remember, your baby has ears that already love listening to your voice!

Sing Along

Change the lyrics to a popular song or a classic children's song, adding your baby's name as you sing along.

"The eensy weensy *Johnny* went up the water spout. Down came the rain and washed *him* right out!"

"Twinkle, twinkle, little star, I love Ava near and far."

Make up your own words, or your own song. If you aren't ready to reveal the baby's name yet, use a nickname as you sing.

Belly Massage

Use your fingers and hands to gently rub your belly, using lotion if you prefer. Imagine that you are lovingly massaging your calm energy into your baby. Swoop around the curves of your belly and growing baby. Move slowly and calmly and repeat as many times as you like. You will begin to feel your baby's movements between 18 and 23 weeks. At about 23 weeks, you will be able to see the baby's movements on the surface of your belly. When you feel that little elbow or foot knocking from the inside, give it a little rub from the outside.

Good Morning/Good Night

Make up a special routine just for the start of each morning and the end of each day. It could be a spoken phrase, a song, or a special thought. Every time this routine is completed, connection with your baby grows!

Some examples of Good Morning/Good Night rituals:

Say good night to loved ones ("good night Grandma Rose, good night Grampa Jack up in Heaven")

Give 3 kisses

Sing "You Are My Sunshine"

Learn a New Tune

Lullabies and nursery rhymes are a simple way to share calm connection, and even to create a routine. Pick one that you loved as a child and sing it to your baby. Your baby can hear sounds outside of the womb starting at about 19 weeks. Whether or not you can carry a tune, your voice will always be music to your baby's ears!

Not familiar with rhymes or lullabies? No problem: Look online for ideas. This website is also a useful resource www.parents.com/baby/sleep/tips/nursery-rhymes-lullabies/

Flashlight Game

Amazingly, your baby can see light outside of the womb—through the skin of your belly—beginning around 15 weeks of pregnancy. Around the time when you can feel baby's movements, put her sight to the test with this fun game. Turn off the lights and shine a flashlight on a part of your belly. Wait for your baby to respond, then move the light to a different spot and see what happens. Notice if there are different responses as your pregnancy progresses.

Tickle Time

You will be able to see movement from outside of your belly around 23 weeks. When baby is kicking and flipping, join in the fun: Tickle Time! Tickle your belly where you feel the movements. How does your baby respond? Playfully talk to your baby as you tickle or make up a tickle song. This is a game that you'll be able to play for years, tickling your newborn gently and your future one-, two-, three-, four-, and five- year-old with more and more energy and excitement.

Heartbeat Keepsake

By 12 weeks of pregnancy, you can hear your baby's heartbeat; record this wonderful sound on your phone. Listen to the recording when you need a pick-me-up, or when you just want to connect with your baby. Share the sound with your loved ones. Play this recording to remind yourself of your growing baby, and of all the amazing changes going on inside of you.

Heart to Heart

You can hear your baby's heartbeat by 12 weeks of pregnancy, and he can hear your heartbeat by 19 weeks. Find a quiet moment and place one hand on your heart and another on the center of your belly; take some deep, relaxing breaths. Feel and recognize the strength of your heart to support the growth of your baby's heart.

Thankful

Close your eyes, take a deep breath, and think of one pregnancy-related thing you are thankful for. Surround your baby with all of the positive energy that feeling gratitude brings.

Sometimes it is a challenge to find the positive in pregnancy. It can be a time of much joy, but also of worry. It can bring feelings of confidence and strength, but also soreness, discomfort, and sickness. Some days this exercise will be easy, and some days it may feel impossible. Take time to find one positive thing, no matter how tiny.

I Spy Happiness

Look for signs of happiness all around you, wherever you are. Anything goes: a leaf waving in the wind, a tail-wagging dog, a couple holding hands . . . Challenge yourself to find people, sounds, and things in your environment that make you feel happy. Imagine surrounding your baby with happiness, no matter where you happen to be.

Snack Time

Everything you eat and drink goes into the healthy growth and development of your baby; pick a healthy snack and enjoy it together.

Talk about what you are eating to bring another level of connection between you and your baby. Even in the womb, your baby is taking in tastes, sounds, and sights.

Read to Me

Your baby can hear sounds outside of the womb starting at about 19 weeks and will be able to recognize your voice when he's born. Find a book that you enjoy and read it out loud to your baby. Inexpensive children's books can be found at drugstores and grocery stores, or you can look for free ones at doctor visits or in community centers (of course, the library has free books, as well). The key is for your baby to hear your voice.

Love Paint

Pretend your hands are paintbrushes, and gently caress your belly. Tell your baby that you are painting her with love. Make sure to apply lots and lots of love paint (not real paint) so your baby really feels it!

Try other kinds of paint, too. Maybe your baby needs Healthy Paint if you're not feeling so good, or Happy Paint, to relax with happy thoughts. Pretending to "paint" your baby with love, health, or happiness creates a calm atmosphere in which both you and your baby can relax.

Affirmation Game

Sit in front of a mirror with your hands around your baby (on the sides of your belly). With excitement and positive energy, call out the wonderful things about your baby, and about yourself as a mother-to-be, such as:

You are growing so healthy and strong!

You will grow up to do anything you set your mind on!

I am doing my best to take care of you.

Try this when your mood is already positive, to highlight your good feelings. Also try this when your mood is low, to see if you can make yourself feel better.

Here are some other good examples of affirmations:

You are loved.

You are safe.

I love myself, and I love you.

I am kind and loving.

We are brave.

We are joyful.

I am proud of myself.

Our bodies are strong and healthy.

You make me smile.

You have so many people who love you.

I am strong, inside and out.

You get smarter and stronger every day.

Drumline

Use your belly as your drum and feel the beat! Gently drum along to songs on your phone or make your own music. Experiment with how it sounds and feels to tap on different parts of your belly. Notice any reaction from your baby, too.

How Big Am I Growing?

Use random items to measure your growing belly, such as a spatula, a dandelion, or a shoe. Hold the item against your belly and work your way around as you count higher and higher. "Wow, Baby, you're 4 cell phones big already!" Be sure to measure again at a later time to see how much your baby has grown.

Rock-a-Bye Baby

Hold your belly and rock your body, just as you will once your baby is born. Sing or hum a favorite lullaby. Set a calm mood by being slow and gentle.

Sing and Squeeze

Select a familiar children's song, such as "The Wheels on the Bus," "Itsy Bitsy Spider," or "Row, Row, Row Your Boat." Sing the song to your baby while adding touch to match the lyrics.

For example: "The wheels on the bus go round and round, round and round, round and round all through the town." (During this verse, you might make a circular motion on your belly and a simple clap pattern for the town). "The horn on the bus goes beep, beep, beep, beep, beep, beep, beep, beep, beep, all through the town." (Push on your belly button for the beeps and repeat a simple clap pattern for town).

Sing the songs the usual way or add your own variations and lyrics. Pay attention to your baby's response, especially after about 18 weeks, when you can feel your baby move. Another variation is to match your pace, tone, and intensity to the situation: calm and slow at bedtime, or with lots of energy when you're trying to get going for the day.

I Love You More

This activity is a take on the children's book *Guess How Much I Love You*, by Sam McBratney and Anita Jeram. The love you have with your baby is growing every day, so spend some time describing it!

"I love you more than all the stars in the sky."

"I love you more than all the candy at Halloween."

"I love you more than all the cars on this street."

Goodnight Touch

Tell your baby a story, while at the same time "drawing" the story on your belly with your finger. For example, tell a story about a puppy and pretend to draw a puppy on your belly. Tell your baby how much you love him and "draw" a heart on your belly with your finger. When your baby is born, you can do this same activity, but drawing gently on your child's back or body. It is similar to scratching someone's back or tickling lightly with your fingers: your touch is gentle, and is meant to feel relaxing.

My Way Superhighway

Find a toy and hop on the highway—your belly! Screech around tight turns, like elbows; rev your engine at a red light, like your belly button. Peel out and cover the "miles." It's not necessary to use a toy car, or even to use a toy at all. Pretend your finger is a car and zoom it along or make a stuffed animal vroom all around.

For quieter times, "drive" around your belly slowly and gently, with soft sound effects.

Finger Kisses

Use your pointer finger to press gentle kisses all over your belly. Tell your baby how much you love her. Make silly kissing sounds to really seal the deal!

Birdwatching

Look for birds and describe to your baby what you see. Notice how birds dart and swoop, float and flap. Imagine soaring like a bird, so high above the ground, joyful and free.

Get in the habit of spotting birds with your baby. They are common enough to see anywhere, and they might become special symbols of your love. As your baby grows up, you will share this special symbol. Throughout your child's life, when he sees a bird, he'll think of you.

On This Day

Record pop culture events happening throughout your pregnancy and on the day your baby is born: the song always playing on the radio, sports championship winners, news stories, or anything else important to you. You will enjoy looking back on what was happening during this time of your life

Future

These activities are all about the days and years to come: routines and traditions, goals and dreams for you, your baby, and your family.

Imagine . . .

Take some time to focus on your dreams and desires for your baby. Imagine the near future, such as a healthy birth, and how it will feel to finally get to hold your baby. Think about who you'd like to have with you in your labor and delivery. Or simply imagine the tiny t-shirts you've purchased being worn by your actual baby.

You might also imagine your baby in the distant future, starting kindergarten, then college. Imagining big goals is the first step toward achieving them!

What If . . .

This activity is similar to Imagine but with a twist: In this activity, you must imagine that your child makes choices that are challenging for you (but aren't objectively negative). For example, Cavaliers fans who get a kid who is a Warriors fan. Or Ohio State parents whose kid goes to rival Michigan.

What allegiances run deep in your family? What food, animal, or toy do you really want your child to love, that he'll end up rejecting for its opposite?

Here are some other examples:

What if your child will only eat broccoli (and the smell of it makes you sick)?

What if your child cries when she hears your favorite song?

What if you're deathly afraid of spiders but your child gets one for a pet? (It's OK to be ridiculous in this activity—have fun coming up with scenarios, whether they could really happen or not!)

Mom Power

What is your Mom Power, or special skill you will bring to motherhood? Are you an excellent toy-organizer? Do you need very little sleep? Do you love playing endless repetitive games? Can you listen to children's music without getting cranky? If you answered yes to any of these questions, you have a Mom Power! All mothers find some aspects of motherhood to be simple and fun and (many) others to be boring or difficult. When everybody else's challenge is easy for you, that's your Mom Power. What are your Mom Powers?

Lifelines

In game shows, when a contestant is stuck on a question, they call their lifeline for help. Who is your lifeline? Think of a person in your life who you can call when times are hard. A friend, family member, or community support who listens or helps can be a lifesaver during long, lonely days.

Teacher

Think of at least one thing that you want to teach your baby someday. Ideas include: an activity or sport; something you learned from your own mother as a child; your family heritage or native language. Write down your ideas and start planning for how and when you'll share your wisdom with your child.

Pick a Value

Identify one or two of your most important beliefs, such as honesty, compassion, gratitude, hard work, or education. Think about how you can instill those values in your child. For example, if you value optimism, you can make a point to model optimism when times are hard (Tell your child, "I had a hard day today, but tomorrow is another chance"). If you value education, make a plan for supporting your child in school (Commit to helping your child with homework, attending teacher conferences, volunteering in the classroom).

A child's parents are his or her first (and best) teachers. Live by your values, and your child will, too.

Values:

- Assertiveness
- Bravery
- Compassion
- Confidence
- Creativity
- Determination
- Exploration
- Family
- Generosity
- Gratitude
- Hope
- Hard work
- Honesty
- Healthiness
- Humor
- Imagination
- Joy
- Love
- Learning
- Optimism
- Persistence
- Self-reliance
- Strength
- Toughness

Traditions

Think of a tradition that you would like to start. Birthdays, holidays, first day of summer, or some random day that only your family celebrates—have fun coming up with a special way to mark the day.

Examples of birthday traditions:

- make paper cut-outs of your child's age and place them around the house—there's a 2 on the floor, the cereal bowl, the bathroom mirror, and the couch!
- take a photo with the same stuffed animal every year
- sing the birthday song in a special way
- special birthday meal
- write a note to the birthday child to tell him what you're proud of

Examples of holiday traditions:

- make homemade decorations together
- get together with extended family
- take a family photograph

Examples of random traditions:

- eat popsicles on the first day of summer
- write a special note to your child on the first day of school
- always give a special hug and kiss when you say goodbye

Sibling Plan

Come up with a plan during pregnancy for how you'll help members of your household adjust to life with the new baby. How will the new siblings meet? Does your roommate know how much newborns cry? Research some ideas online and be sure to share the plan with the members of your household.

Pet Plan

Come up with a plan during pregnancy for how you'll help your pet accept the new baby. Check with your vet for tips, and research some ideas online.

Some ideas to get you started:

- Before the baby comes home from the hospital, bring a blanket with his scent home for the pet to smell.
- Keep the baby's room or crib off-limits from pets
- Make the first meeting of baby and pet a calm and relaxed moment. Be mindful of the pet's reactions. Don't forget to give some love to your pet; remember that pets have feelings, too.

Me and My Shadow

Picture yourself in the future, hanging out with your little shadow. What do you love to do that you can do with your child one day? Baking cookies, shoe shopping, cheering on your favorite sports team, dressing alike . . . You and your shadow!

Positive Personality Predictions

Imagine that your baby ends up with the best personality traits of you and your partner. Identify each of your top 5 traits.

Now and Then

If your pregnancy habits influenced your baby's personality, what would that look like? For example, if you crave Italian food every day, will your baby speak Italian? If you spend your pregnancy binge watching Netflix, will your baby become a movie star? Have fun matching your pregnancy habits with your baby's future personality or career.

Going Home with Baby

Plan ahead for the hospital, and for one day bringing your baby home. Pack a bag for yourself, with clothes, toiletries, and personal items. Get the car seat ready and pack a diaper bag with supplies. Have fun picking out an outfit for your baby to wear home.

Three Wishes

Send three wishes to your baby. For example: You will experience joyful laughter every day; you will be safe and happy; you will learn to vacuum at a very young age. It's not important that each wish be realistic or serious. Just enjoy the process of thinking about the future with your baby.

Goodnight Touch

Start practicing this simple routine now by telling your baby a bedtime story and, at the same time, use your finger to "draw" the story on your belly.

Activities for Birth to Age 6

Apple Pie

Get ready to gobble up a sweet, delicious treat: your child! First, chop up some apples (Use the sides of your hands to chop, chop, chop on your child's body). Then, sprinkle on some cinnamon (Use your fingertips to lightly tap your child's head, ears, and shoulders). Pour on some sugar (Cover your child in real kisses or "finger kisses," where you use your pointer fingers and kissing sounds to touch your child's face, torso, and toes)! Put the pie in the oven (Fold your child into a great, big hug). Notice how good it smells while it bakes (exaggerated sniffs of your child's head, neck, etc., with exclamations of deliciousness). And then, of course, eat that pie up! So yummy!

Balance Beam

Hold your child's hand and help him walk on top of a curb or a low wall. Your child can try to walk on his own while you cheer him on! For a fun twist, your child can jump off into your arms, or can hold your hand while walking on the curb.

Be My Baby

Hold your young child on your lap while you bounce, tilt, and tip her around, making silly faces and exciting sounds. You can also challenge her to balance on your lap while you move her around without the support of your arms.

Beep Game

Touch different body parts on your child while making silly noises. Let your child do the same to you. Be creative with your sounds, and remember that an excited voice and animated gestures make all the difference. If your child is slow to reciprocate the touch/sound cycle, try changing the volume or tone of your voice to increase or decrease the energy of the interaction. Think of cartoon sound effects if you need ideas: *zip, bong, bam, pow, zoom, wheeee!*

The Big Sneeze

Put an object on your head—a sock, a stuffed animal, or a soft toy—and build up for a big sneeze: Ah, ah, ah, AH CHOO! Send the object flying from your head.

Boom Shush

Take turns identifying things that are loud and quiet. Copy the noises, or just use a loud voice and a quiet voice. This is a great activity for teaching kids to whisper.

"Car horns are loud: Beep beep! Blankie is quiet."

"Fireworks are loud: Bang, pop, boom! Butterflies are quiet."

"Monkeys are loud: Ooh, ooh, ooh, ah, ah, ah! Kittens are quiet: Meow."

Brave Balancing

Use your imagination to pretend your child is walking along a tricky path or tightrope. "You're walking along a cliff, and you're way up in the mountains. Don't fall onto the sharp rocks below!" Build the excitement while you take turns imagining different parts of the journey. "Walk carefully so you don't fall! Watch out for that eagle—it has sharp talons!" Have your child walk an imaginary or taped line safely back to your embrace.

Burrito Baby

Who's hungry? Let's make burritos! Place a blanket on the floor and have your child lie on top. Load your "burrito" up with all sorts of yummy toppings by touching, rubbing, and patting your hands on your child's belly, head, arms, and legs. "Here are the beans . . . Here's the cheese . . . Now comes the salsa . . ." Try to cover your child's whole body in pretend ingredients. Add some ice cream or other silly ingredients to really make your child giggle.

Once all of the toppings have been added, wrap your child up in the blanket just like a burrito. Massage your child from shoulders to toes while talking or singing about the delicious burrito baby, then pretend to gobble your burrito up!

Chew Chew

It's dinner time, here comes the Chew Chew Train! All aboard! The first train car is peas. Mush, mush, mush, chew those peas up. Next is carrots: crunch, crunch, crunch. Chugga chugga chew chew! Here comes the milk! Slurp, slurp, slurp! Add as many trains cars and sounds as you need. You'll hear giggles, and your child will probably get a few more bites of vegetables.

Extreme Peek-a-Boo

Disappear behind a chair or door, then pop out with an exaggerated expression. Disappear again, and pop out with a completely different expression. Playfully act out different emotions, and if your child seems interested, have him guess which feeling you are showing. Make sure your child understands that you are playing a game, and that you aren't really feeling mad or sad or scared. This is a great opportunity to talk with your child about different feelings.

Fee, Fi, Fo, Fum, Look Out, Baby, Here I Come!

Use your child's name instead of "Baby" in this chant, and call it out while you walk slowly toward your child, arms outstretched, ready to tickle and hug. Your child may gleefully run away, hoping you'll chase after. If you're not feeling that energetic, keep your own pace slow. Let your child figure out that the fun is in the hugging and tickling time. When you're feeling energetic, pick up the pace.

Finger Man

Here comes Finger Man! Use your pointer finger and index finger to create Finger Man's legs and have him dance, run, and jump around. Finger man may even jump onto your child and start some tickle time! Or maybe he's going to run and check out that salad on your plate—yum! What will he do next? What will your child's Finger Man do? Better find out! Maybe the two Finger Friends can take an adventure together.

Food Fables

At mealtime, make up a story about the food you are eating. Use real ideas or imaginary ones to amplify your child's interest, and to create an experience of togetherness as you taste different flavors. You might talk about the foods that ballerinas eat after they dance, or about trucks taking lettuce to the grocery store, or busy bees making the honey that goes on your child's toast.

"This crunchy apple tastes so sweet! I think the sun came out and warmed up the farmer's field. The apple tree opened up its branches to feel the sun, and the apples grew *this* big!"

It's not important to focus on the accuracy of the information that you and your child share; instead, focus on the fable you create together.

Food Guessing

Guess what's for lunch, just by smell! Hold a plate of food near your child's nose and see if your child can figure it out. Eyes closed, of course!

Food Zoo

Pretend that there are animals on your child's plate, not food. "Looks like you have crocodiles for dinner! And hippos! Yum, yum, I love those! Which will you eat first?" Add animal noises and funny faces for more fun.

Freeze It

Take a cold object (an ice cube, a sippy cup, or anything else that works) and touch it to a spot on your child's body. Then use a soft towel and your hands to massage warmth back into that spot. Pick another spot and repeat. Build excitement by wondering, "Where will the cold spot be next? Your cheek? Your toe? The back of your knee?"

Is it really cold? Well, warm it up, Buttercup! Let your child take a turn at being the freezer and warmer, too.

Gumby

Remember Gumby, the green clay character whose body could stre-e-etch? Turn your child into Gumby in this activity! Have your child lie down and hold her arm or leg, bend it slowly in toward her body, then gently stretch it out straight. Wrap your fingers around her arm or leg and pull your hands along, over and over, like a massage. When one leg is nice and long, move to the other leg. Make sure you stretch her out really, really long! If it seems fun, throw in a song: "This is the way we stretch our legs, stretch our legs, stretch our legs, this is the way we stretch our legs so they are nice and long."

Heart Check-In

Tune in to the quiet mood of your child, which sometimes leads to sadness or upset, but can easily get lost in the shuffle of busy days. Do a Heart Check-In so your child knows that you notice her, and that you accept her different feelings. Place your hand on her heart and say what you notice: "Your eyes look sad and your mouth is down. How is your heart?" You may offer a prompt, such as, "Sometimes when my eyes look like yours, I feel sad." Use this for all feelings, not just sadness. Sometimes our anger and our fear come from a hurt heart. Don't forget to do a Heart Check-In for happy hearts, too!

Heart Hide 'N' Seek

Cut out fabric or paper hearts, and take turns hiding them in a small area. Hearts can be about the size of your child's hand, although younger children might enjoy finding larger hearts, and older children might like the challenge of finding smaller hearts. When you find each heart, celebrate with hugs and kisses.

Adjust the challenge according to the age of your child, and remember that the goal is to celebrate together, not to make an impossible task. For your 2- to 3-year-old, place a heart on top of your child's teddy bear's head or on a couch cushion. In a typical living room, this will be tricky enough. For your 5- to 6-year-old, hiding the heart under a favorite toy or under the TV stand would be appropriate. Older children enjoy verbal clues: "You're getting warmer. Now you're getting colder." Get creative, get silly, and remember to struggle a little bit to find the heart that your child "hides" in the middle of the floor!

Hold Up the Wall

Is your child too full of energy, having a hard time keeping her body still and her hands to herself? Quick, see if she can help you hold up that shaky wall!

Put your palms on the wall and push, push, push! Don't let the wall fall down!

Hot Chocolate

This activity borrows from Apple Pie and Burrito, but is short and sweet(!) and useful for flipping your child's mood or ending power struggles. The hot chocolate (your child) is hot, hot, hot! "Ouch, too hot to touch!" Cool it down (blow gently on your child's hair, neck, and hands). Sprinkle in some marshmallows (tap fingers gently on your child's head). "Can I touch you now? Almost!" Repeat. Your child decides when she is cool enough to touch and to "drink." Hug and snuggle. Drink her up! Mmmmm. Delicious!

Hurt Finder

Take turns being the Hurt Finder, looking closely at each other's arms, legs, fingers, ears, nose, and toes to find the places that hurt.

This game lets you get very silly ("Any hurts on your teeth? In your armpit?") but could also be a chance to look for emotional hurts ("Any hurts in your heart? In your thoughts?").

Change the pace of the game to match the mood you're trying to achieve. At bedtime, you will want to slow the pace and use gentle touch and movements.

After a real hurt happens—for example, if your child just wiped out on the sidewalk—take the time to hold your child close and really look at the sore knee (or whatever). Then look for other places that got

hurt in the tumble. Chances are great that the pain your child feels—
and the tears—will go away faster if you really focus on your child's
need. This is also the case with those "emotional hurts" that children
feel, but usually can only express with tears, tantrums, or other be-
haviors (which end up eliciting adult irritation, not connection and
empathy).

If your child is having a bad day, or if the tears and "No!'s" just keep
on coming, this game might soothe the emotional pain. The problems and the scraped knees (and all the silly pretend hurts) will still
be there, but your child will feel supported and loved. Isn't everything
easier with support and love?

Invisible Balance Beam

"Draw" an invisible balance beam with your finger, and ask your
child to walk, jump, hop, or roll across while keeping her balance.
Use the floor tiles of the grocery store, or sidewalk lines. If you have
masking tape, put a line of it on the floor. Outside, draw a chalk line.
Make up different challenges, and cheer on your child's effort.

Kid Bridge

Your child is the bridge between two family members and gets to
carry the love from one side of the bridge to the other. Carry hugs,
kisses, or a special message from one person to another. Tell your
child what kind of love to share, or let your child decide. Take turns
being the bridge.

Kid Tug o' War

Your child is the rope, and you and another family member "battle"
to win the tug o' war so you can hold, hug, kiss, and snuggle your
child first! Take turns winning this game and being the rope, to really
spread the joy.

This game works well with any three people. Siblings are wonderful
because this game teaches playful strength and aggression. You can
model the playful, gentle struggle for the chance to win the love game.
When the sibling wins the tug o' war, kids get to practice joyful touch

(versus angry touch, which comes all too easily to most kids). Onlookers can pour on praise and high fives after someone wins.

Let's Take a Trip

Where should we go today? You and your child take an imaginary trip, such as to the barber shop or nail salon. Talk about all the things that will happen on your trip and use playful, gentle touch to act them out on your child.

For example: "Do you want to take a trip to the barber shop? First, we put on the cape to keep your body dry." (Pretend to wrap a cape around your child's chest and neck.) "Then, we lay your head back in the sink and wash your hair." (Begin giving a head massage). "Next, we dry your hair with a towel. Now it's time for the scissors, chop, chop, chop." Proceed with the steps until your trip to the barber shop comes to an end.

Other trip ideas: car wash, makeup store, tattoo parlor. The variations are endless. Use your own and your child's interests and experiences. Remember, it's all about being together and feeling the joy of the moment!

Love Paint

Pretend your hands are paintbrushes, and gently caress your child's face, shoulders, head, arms, and legs. Tell your child that you are painting her with love. Make sure to apply lots and lots of love paint so your child really feels it!

Try other kinds of paint, too. Maybe your child needs Brave Paint before going on a play date at a new friend's house, or Happy Paint, to go to bed with happy thoughts.

What kind of paint do you need today? Have your child paint you with Patience Paint, Smart Paint, or Silly Paint.

Mirror Game

Be your child's "mirror" by imitating her facial expressions, body movements, and postures. Take turns being the mirror and the mover. Make big moves, like stretching way up tall, and little moves, like just making your eyebrows wiggle up and down. Make exaggerated frowns and smiles, or make worried, excited, or bored faces. See if your mirror can even copy your dance moves!

My Way Superhighway

Find a toy and hop on the highway—your child's body! Screech around tight turns, like elbows; rev your engine at a red light, like her belly button. Peel out and cover the "miles." It's not necessary to use a toy car, or even to use a toy at all. Pretend your finger is a car and zoom it along, or make a stuffed animal vroom all around.

For quieter times, "drive" around your child's body slowly and gently, with soft sound effects or simply naming body parts (ankles, eyelids, shins—there are so many interesting body parts to name). Time to take a drive to earlobe island!

One, Two, Stack-A-Roo

See what you can stack on your head, and how high you can go! How many books, small blocks, or pillows can you each stack on your own heads or on each other's heads before the items fall off?

Pass It On!

Sit face to face with your child, or in a circle if there are more people. One person starts the game by touching the next person in a special way; that person passes along the same touch to the next person, and so on. When it gets back to the first person, start the game again with a new leader, or try a new way of touching. This is an excellent game for families to teach and practice gentle and respectful touch.

Some ideas for starting the game: Use your finger or toe (or even your nose!). Touch elbows, foreheads, knees. Pass along a hug or a kiss, a high five, or a special handshake.

Pip, Pip, Pop!

Similar to Duck, Duck, Goose, but with a hug and a kiss instead of a run around the circle. Say, "Pip, pip, pip, POP!" On "pop," your child jumps up to hug and kiss you. Create excitement by varying how many "pips" you add. You can also vary your pace, speaking very slowly at times and quickly at others. Remember to take turns being the pipper and the popper. This is a good activity for building action and energy, and so might not be best at bedtime or relaxing time.

Red Light, Green Light

Encourage listening and self-control by adding fun twists to this classic game. Pretend to be different vehicles as you travel through the school. Add stoplight commands:

Red Light = stop. Green Light = go. Yellow Light = slow down.

For example, "Today we're mail trucks, delivering the mail to our house. Green light, let's go."

Feel free to substitute characters from books, or animals, or sports heroes for vehicles.

Rock-a-Bye Baby

Pretend your child is still a little baby. Hold him in your arms and rock. Sing or hum a favorite lullaby. Set a silly mood by using a fast pace and more animated voice, or a calm mood by being slow and gentle.

Rocking Hugs

Hugs with rhythm. Use your whole body to hug and rock, just like when your child was a baby. Imagine you are sending all your loving feelings into your child, and imagine your child is absorbing all that love like a sponge—because that *is* what is happening!

Show Me Your Muscles

Which muscles are you working on today: Your thinking muscles? Your friendship muscles? Your happy muscles? Show me how big they are! Have your child flex his arms and give his muscles a squeeze.

Keep working on different muscles so they get bigger and bigger. Be sure to tell your child when you notice that his work is paying off:

"Wow, your sitting-still muscles are looking good today! Let me see you flex! Keep up the good work!"

Sing and Squeeze

Select a familiar children's song, such as "The Wheels on the Bus," "Itsy Bitsy Spider," or "Row, Row, Row Your Boat." Sing the song with your child while adding touch to match the lyrics.

For example: "Let's jump on the bus and sing! The wheels on the bus go round and round, round and round, round and round all through the town." (During this verse, you might make a circular motion on a part of your child's body, like belly, back or head for wheels and a simple clap pattern for the town). "The horn on the bus goes beep, beep, beep, beep, beep, beep, beep, beep, beep, all through the town." (Push on your child's belly button or nose for the beeps and repeat a simple clap pattern for town).

Sing the songs the usual way or add your own variations and lyrics. Pay attention to your child's experience and make adjustments if necessary. Match your pace, tone, and intensity to the situation: calm and slow at bedtime, or with lots of energy when you're trying to improve your child's mood.

Smelly Chef

While you cook, talk about the different smells you notice. Sniff the ingredients. See which smells your child likes and dislikes. Use a daily chore, cooking, to have fun with your child in a whole new way.

Sneaky Sticker

Show your child some "special stickers" that you'll only use with her. Tell her that you are going to hide a few around your home, just for her to find. Make a plan that when she finds the sticker she needs to celebrate with you. Be sure to celebrate the connection that you are building—how exciting to find the Sneaky Sticker, and to know that you are thinking of her!

Sniff & Snuggle

Find some things with a nice scent, like lotion, vanilla, or perfume. Dab some on a cotton ball or on your child's skin. Snuggle your child close as you enjoy the sensations of touch and scent. Bring these sensations to your child's awareness by taking big breaths through your nose. "You feel so good in my arms, and the lemony smell makes me feel so happy inside."

Sock Surprise

Put a secret object in a sock and ask your child to guess what it is. No peeking; just stick your hand inside and figure it out by feel. Ideas for objects: a coin, a small toy, a spoon, a rock. Kids love to be surprised, and you can build the excitement with your facial expressions and tone of voice. They also love to give surprises, so switch roles and let your child pick the secret object. Don't forget to make silly guesses (Is it a rhinoceros in the sock?).

Steamroller

Like rolling down a hill, but flat! Have your child lie down in an open area of the floor or on a bed. Roll your child around like a log or like a steamroller, pushing on shoulders and hips. Add noises or "danger" for joyful effect: "There's a big rock in the road! Let's roll, roll, roll! We flattened it!" Take turns being the roller and the rolled.

You can also try this lying down, with your child lying across your chest. Steamroll your child all the way down your own body to your toes (sitting up when needed). Then roll your child all the way back up!

Stinky Tootsies

Smell your child's feet and makes exaggerated *pee-eew* sounds. How does her neck smell? Her arms? Explore her body, making sure to make yummy sounds sometimes, too. "That cute belly smells like delicious pumpkin pie!"

Stop 'n' Go

This variation on Tickle Time is wonderful for building your child's sense of trust in you. Tickle until your child says "stop." Then, wait for your child to say "go" before tickling again.

You can also play Stop 'n' Go with other kinds of touch, such as soft brushing, or squeezing your child's hands, feet, or arms. Try it with wrestling, then cuddling, or with fast then slow. The key is that your child is in control of the game.

Highly active play can be challenging because many children have difficulty calming down afterward. Stop 'n' Go allows for some breaks in the action, so your child can practice calming down when all revved up.

Tasty Copy Cat

Encourage your picky eater by playing a copying game while you share a meal. Let's take a bite of rice, mmmmm! Make a funny face while you chew, and have your child make the same face with his own bite of food. Add lots of enthusiasm. Get more food in his belly by letting him choose the food and the face that you must copy!

Word Mirror (variation on Mirror Game)

Sit face to face with your child and pretend you're a Word Mirror—use your words to describe what you see: "I see gorgeous brown eyes, a tulip mouth, and springy hair." Identify the wonderful traits your child has: "I see your big, huge brain and your thoughtful words," or get silly, "I see puppy dog ears and kittycat whiskers!" Take turns, so your child can practice observing and describing, and making up fun ideas of her own.

If your child is having big feelings, use Word Mirror to help your child understand ("I see angry eyebrows and a frowny mouth. I see big, mad feelings, and some sad ones, too"). Remember to honor big feelings, not make light of them. When you use a gentle, calm voice and have a relaxed body, your child is more likely to calm down and relax, too.

Activities for Ages 6–12

Air Drawing

Stand face to face with your child and take turns drawing different object in the air, using your pointer finger. Feel free to establish a category before the game begins (animals, classroom objects, food, etc.) See who can guess the most right!

And the Kid's Choice Award Goes To . . .

Ask your child about his all-time favorite movie and character. Prompt him to announce the Choice Award for that character.

Brag Board

Ask your child to put together a "brag board". The board can include things that he wants to brag about. Help your child brainstorm and be sure he thinks about bragging for being (who he is and things he likes) and bragging for doing (achievements, accomplishments). The Brag Board doesn't have any limit to size; it could be something as small as an index card to as large as a poster board—the possibilities are endless.

Brag Call

Celebrate your child's accomplishments, no matter how big or small. Has your child been struggling to get a good grade on a test, or forgetting to do something around the house? Next time he gets a good grade on a test, make a call to a family member or friend to "brag" about his accomplishment.

Brain Massages

Is your child struggling to stay focused? Maybe she needs a "stay focused" brain massage. Give her a "sitting still brain massage." To be brave on the slide? Time for a "bravery" brain massage. Just use your fingers and palm to gently rub your child's forehead, being sure to tell her exactly what's being rubbed into her brain. "I can see it's hard for you to sit still. I'm giving you a brain massage. I'm rubbing in a whole bunch of sitting-still, so you can do it on your own."

Doodle

Use a small notebook to pass back and forth between you and your child. Draw a doodle on a page and hand the notebook to your child to create something out of the doodle. Repeat as many times as you can.

Dreamy

You and your child write a hope/wish/dream on a small piece of paper. You both can share anything, whether or not it can really happen. This gives both of you the opportunity to think about and share the joy you hope to experience in the future.

Fun Fact of the Day

Ask your child to share with you one "fun fact" about him. If he has a hard time thinking of a fun fact to share, here are some questions that you can prompt him with: Favorite food you ate today? Favorite hobby (scouts, karate, collecting rocks, dancing, or singing)? You could ask about one fun fact from his day at school or for the whole week. Encourage your child to ask you, too. Have fun with this one, and try not to assume you have all the facts.

Guess the Instrument

Pretend to play an instrument while the other one guesses which instrument is being played. A variation could be "guess the sport" or another other interest that you think would be fun.

Hangman

Use a small notebook to pass back and forth between you and your child. Anyone can initiate a game of Hangman using positive characteristics or traits or compliments. This is a time for connection and praise.

High/Low

Ask your child about her high and low for the past 24 hours – something that she was successful doing and something she wishes she could "do over" or that she could have done differently. Be sure to share yours, too!

Humpty Dumpty Fix

Humpty Dumpty sat on the wall. Humpty Dumpty had a great fall. . .

Did your child just get hurt or feel a disappointment? Say the nursery rhyme while taking care of your child. Pat and hug and gently rub the hard feelings out. Put Humpty Dumpty back together again.

Imaginary Baseball

Baseball with a twist! Take turns being the pitcher and the batter. The pitcher will "throw" an imaginary ball to the batter and the batter will swing their arms to "knock it out of the park." To make the game even more exciting, take turns narrating the plays as you go ("Here, batter, batter!" "HOME RUN!").

Lather Up

Grab some scented lotion and give your child the opportunity to apply it to hands and arms or you can apply it on each other. If possible, it's nice to have lotions that have a relaxing and calming smell.

Letter Game

Pick a positive descriptive word starting with the first letter of your child's first name. Come up with as many as possible. If your child is old enough, challenge him to return the love. This is another way to share joy with positive words.

Scramble

Scramble a positive word on paper and have your child figure out the word. Take turns so that you both get to hear something positive!

Secret Word

Create a secret word and a silly thing to do when you hear it. "Today's secret word is 'pizza.' If you hear the word 'pizza,' give me a big hug." Once your child understands this silly game, she can help come up with the next code word. At the end of the day, give your child lots of love and praise for how many times she correctly heard you say the code word.

Sleepy Countdown

Calmly and quietly count down from 20 while you rub sleepy thoughts and good feelings into your child's back. Let him know that when you reach zero the back rub is over, but you'll have rubbed in lots of goodness by then. Of course, you can start your countdown at any number. If your child wants you to start at 50, go for it (just count a little faster). The key is to make your body and your voice as calm as possible to send that quiet sleepy message to your child.

Special Soup

Create a fake soup with your child. What is something that's important to your child? Friendship or love? Create a soup representing that thing. Your child might want to create a friendship soup filled with kindness, honesty, and loyalty. Have fun adding the ingredients that make up whatever is important in that moment!

Story Builder

Take turns telling a story, one sentence at a time. For example, you might say, "Once there was a boy with a pet bear." The child might say, "They went to school." You continue the story, keeping it fun and on track. Starting with a silly first sentence is a good way to build the joy. Here are some silly story starter ideas, just to get your creative juices flowing:

"One day I went to Mars and I saw the most amazing things."

"My brother is an octopus and he loves to play games with me."

"Once there was a girl who could catch butterflies on her nose."

Trust Walk

Take turns closing your eyes and being led through a room or across a low "balance beam" made of blocks or books. Talk about the meaning of trust, and how we depend on each other to be safe and healthy. Provide lots of reassurance through touch and encouraging words. Model for your child how to make another person feel safe. Emphasize the joy by celebrating successful walks and safe landings with lots of hugs and kisses!

Variation: Trust Fall—Have your child closes his or her eyes and fall backwards into your arms. Be sure to make the catch!

Two Truths and a Fib

Have your child tell you 2 truths and 1 fib, and then you have to figure out which one is the fib. Now switch and allow your child to guess your fib. Feel free to get as silly as you want with this one and maybe learn something new about each other!

Warm and Fuzzy

Remind your child to pat herself on the back and or give herself a hug. Demonstrate to your child how to wrap your arms around and give yourself a big hug. This can also be a time for your child to give herself praise and remind herself that she is lovable.

What's Missing?

Select a few interesting objects around you and set them up together. Name each object for your child ("spoon, napkin, salt"), then have her close her eyes. Take one thing away, and ask your child to figure out what's missing. The younger your child is, the fewer the objects you should use. Start small, so your child feels confident. Switch roles and let your child be in charge.

Model strategies for better remembering, like repeating the list of objects. You can also model behavior, such as thinking carefully before giving up and staying calm if you don't know the answer.

Who's on First?

Create signals (think of a third base coach signalling a batter, or a catcher signalling a pitcher) you two can use back and forth between each other.

Word Search

Create a word search specific to your child's strengths, interests, or hobbies. This is a good time to remind your child that you see the good that they do.

AGES 6–12

Activities for All Ages

Affirmation Game

Stand face to face with your child, or with both of you in front of a mirror. With enthusiasm and positive energy, call out the wonderful things about your child: "You believe in yourself! You're healthy and strong! You can do anything you set your mind on!" After each thing that you say, your child repeats it back: "I believe in myself! I'm healthy and strong! I can do anything I set my mind on!"

Here are some other good examples of affirmations:

You are loved.

You are safe.

You are friendly.

You are a good friend.

You are thoughtful.

All of your feelings are OK.

You always do your best.

You are a great listener.

You can learn from your mistakes.

You love yourself.

You are a positive thinker.

You can solve problems.

You are kind and loving.

You are brave.

You are joyful.

You work hard.

You are proud of yourself.

You are a fast learner.

You can help others.

Your body is strong and healthy.

You have so many people who love you.

ALL AGES

You are a good friend.

You have great ideas.

You have a great imagination.

You are strong, inside and out.

You get smarter and stronger every day.

You have a great memory.

You love to share your happiness with others.

You can do it.

The Amazing Invention Game

What's your child struggling with? What kind of cool machine do you wish existed? Wish you could eat buttered noodles for breakfast, lunch, and dinner, but Mom won't let you? You need an Amazing Invention for that: Noodleator!

Create anything in your minds! Traffic got you down? Flying car! Late for school? Magic clock! You want 12 more hugs before bed, but Mom said you're all done? Voila! The Hug and Kiss-erater! You want it, you create it!

Animal Guess Who

Take turns making animal sounds and guessing the animal. Meow like a cat or hiss like a snake. Whistle like a bird. Bark, quack, moo, or hoot. Or play Vehicle Guess Who, with siren, motorcycle, boat, or plane sounds.

Animal Hugs

Pretend you're a koala bear and give your child a great big koala bear hug! How does a koala bear hug? Who knows, so whatever you do will be perfect! Take turns being different animals and give lots of animal hugs.

Animal Kisses

How does a penguin kiss? Who knows, but you're going to figure it out with your child! Pretend to be a waddling penguin as you approach and then cover your child in kisses. Take turns picking animals and sharing animal kisses and hugs. Add a lot of energy and excitement if you need your child to get going, such as before you leave for daycare. Or make it a calming game for bedtime or naptime by quietly sharing animal ideas and love.

Artsy I Spy

Like the classic game of I Spy, but with a modern twist: use a painting, photograph, or page from a magazine. Do you see what I see?

Another variation is to make your own abstract artwork using a blob of paint folded inside a piece of paper. Open the paper and talk about what you see. "I spy a whale!" "I spy a snowman playing baseball!"

Back Stories

Use your child's back as a canvas for invisible writing, painting, or drawing. Tell a story as you draw, or make simple shapes and see if your child can guess what you made. Do a "weather report" on your child by talking about the day—was there sunshine or rain? Was it cloudy? Or talk about different feelings and draw happy/sad/mad faces (This might allow you to calmly process big feelings that child or the parent had that day—but keep things light and fun—no discipline or judgment). Tell a story or draw a nursery rhyme. Make up a story or have your child tell you what to draw. Use other body parts as your canvas, such as your child's cheek, hand, or foot. The possibilities for this activity are endless!

Another variation is Hand Stories, where instead of using your child's back, you use her hand.

Backwards Hugs

Stand back to back with your child and interlace arms. For added fun, count to see how long you can hold the hug. You might need to be on your knees for this one so that you and your child are at similar heights.

ALL AGES

Baking Together

Let your child choose a recipe and make it together. Offer a few simple ideas, like brownies or muffins, and use a boxed mix from the store. If you enjoy baking, use a more complicated recipe, or bake from scratch. The most important part is to include your child in as many steps as possible: dumping in the ingredients, stirring, helping clean up, and of course, enjoying the finished product! No matter how lumpy your cupcakes turn out, if you had fun making them together, it was worth it.

Birdwatching

Take turns looking for birds and describing what you see. Notice how they dart and swoop, float, and flap. Imagine soaring so high above the ground.

Add silly details, like what the birds might do for fun, or what you would do if you could fly with the birds. Pretend the birds are having a party and think about who the guests would be: Chipmunks? Elephants? What games would they play? Hide and seek? Tag?

Get in the habit of spotting birds with your child. They are common enough to see anywhere, and they might become special symbols to your child of your love and care.

Brain Power!

Hold your child's head with both hands and look into her eyes: your words and gaze are going to fill her brain up with power, quick wits, confidence, and love!

"It's Brain Power time! I'm filling your brain up with extra strength and smarts! I'm adding bravery and love! What else do you need in there today? You're smiling, do you need some extra smiles? OK, here they come! You'll have these smiles in there all day, with hugs and kisses, too!"

Breathing Buddies

Use your breath to help your child calm down by becoming Breathing Buddies. Face your child and show her how you take air in and out through your nose and mouth. Ask her to play a game with you in which she copies the way you are breathing. This is a great activity for making your child feel safe as she calms down, because you can use your gaze, your gentle words and touch, and your breath to connect with your child. Make sure to breathe calmly and slowly, and to pace your breathing in a way that your child can copy.

Fast, shallow breathing is counterproductive to calming down, and may cause lightheadedness, so keep it relaxing and joyful (or be ready to switch activities).

Clap It Up

Play classic hand clapping games, like Patty Cake, Miss Mary Mack, or Rockin' Robin, or create one of your own. Are there any clapping games from your childhood that you could teach your child?

Look online for ideas, or if you need a refresher. This website is also a useful resource http://www.todaysparent.com/family/10-classic-hand-clapping-games-to-teach-your-kid/ (active as of May 2017).

Cloud Party

Sit together and watch the clouds "have a party" in the sky. Take turns imagining silly details about the party. Give prompts to spur your child's thinking, or use your child's interests to make the activity even more enjoyable and relatable. If your child loves princesses, send some princesses to that party! What would you do if you were at that party? What would your child do? Follow your child's lead. Build on her ideas. Get creative, get silly, and enjoy the party!

Copy Cat Rhythm

Take turns making and copying the beat. Use taps on your knees, or clap your hands, or just make silly sounds (You say, "Boom, boom, BAM!" and your child says, "Boom, boom, BAM!" back). Make sure you make the beat easy enough for your child to remember and repeat.

ALL AGES

Crazy Laugh Echo

Have a contest to see who can come up with more different "laughs." Laugh back and forth with your child, laughing a different way each time. Each laugh will only last a few seconds. See who can come up with the most, or the silliest laughs.

Dance Party!

Feel the beat; move your hands and feet! Dancing is an excellent way to change the mood from down in the dumps to ready to roll. When you dance, your heart pumps, your body shakes off the tension of the day, and you're primed for laughter and connection with your dance partner.

Did your favorite song just come on the radio while you're driving? It's Dance Party time!

Is your child having a melt down before dinner? It's Dance Party time!

Don't let the lack of a radio stop this party: Imaginary music is just as fun to dance to!

Day at the Zoo

A day at the zoo—what animals do we see? Lions! Pretend to lick your child's face, and brush your child's beautiful mane. Do you see elephants? Wrap your child up in your trunk. What would a shark mom do? Make something up, and go for it!

Don't worry about the accuracy of your grooming techniques, or the fact that your child says she sees ice cream trucks at the zoo, not animals. The sillier the better.

Use this activity to jump start sluggish mornings when you have to get out the door fast and your child is fighting every step. It might be easier to dress a polar bear than a grumpy 4-year-old.

The Director

Your child is the boss in this silly game! The Director calls the shots: Be sad! (You boo-hoo, sniffle, wail, and fall apart.) Be happy! (You instantly switch to being the essence of happiness.) Switch roles from time to time. Be mad! Scared! Nervous! Your child will be laughing while you get to teach different emotion words.

Drumline

Use your child's body as your drum and feel the beat! Drum along to songs on your phone or make your own music. Experiment with how it sounds to tap on your child's hand versus his foot or his shoulder. Let your child tell you where and how you should drum, and then let your child drum on you.

Dry Spaghetti/ Wet Noodle

Use this game to practice shifting energy from active to calm. Call out, "Dry Spaghetti!" and your child stands up straight, tall, and rigid. Say, "Wet Noodle!" and your child goes limp and still. This game is really a sneaky way to practice body awareness, and increases your child's sense of himself in space. You can talk about "making your muscles tight," and "relaxing," concepts that grown-ups understand easily but that children need to be taught. See how fast you both can go to help charge up!

If your family doesn't eat spaghetti, try "Frozen Popsicle/Melted Popsicle" instead.

Earthquake Hug

Hold on tight; it's an earthquake! Hold your child firmly, swaying, jostling, and rattling all around. Don't try this one before bed because it's sure to get your child excited. This might be better for getting a sleepy child started in the morning, or for helping a child to cast off a low or sad mood.

Elbow Kiss

The point of your elbow makes a big smooch as you gently touch the point of your child's elbow. Great for side-by-side activities, such as riding on the bus or sitting together at the table. Did your child just use good manners? Elbow kiss!

ALL AGES

Elevator Hug

Wrap your arms around your child's back (near the waist) and slowly lift him as high as you are able, pretending to be an elevator. Add sound effects or count the floors as you pass them (in your imagination).

Eye Hug

Simply look your child in the eye. Make your eyes "smile" by making your mouth smile. (Try it! You can really feel a difference in your eyes as they soften into a smile). For an extra bonus, bring your foreheads to touch, adding a Forehead Kiss to the mix!

Face Trace

Use your fingers to gently trace your child's face. This is easiest when your child is lying down, so it's great for bedtime, but you can do this anywhere, anytime your child is receptive. Swoop around your child's eyes, along her cheekbones, and over her nose, ears, and mouth. Trace slowly and calmly, and repeat as many times as you like. Talk about the wonderful things you see ("I see your beautiful brown eyes and your curvy eyebrows"). Imagine that you are lovingly tracing your calm energy onto your child.

Finger Hug

Link a single finger and squeeze. Throw in some eye hugs for good measure!

Finger Kiss

Use your pointer finger to press kisses all over your child's face and body. Make a smooch sound to really seal the deal!

Fist Hug

Similar to a Hand Hug, but curl your fingers into fists and hold your child's opposite fist. It looks like you're ready for a Thumb War, but keep the peace—just hug!

ALL AGES

Forehead Kiss

Look your child in the eye while you slowly bring your foreheads to touch.

Forever Hug

Hug your child and try to hold on "forever." The trick is to hold on to the hug way past the point when you would usually stop. (Of course, be sure to stop if your child is not enjoying the game.)

Funny Word Echoes

This is a call-and-response activity in which you and your child take turns saying a funny word. Use different silly voices, and take turns calling and copying. Try using a squeaky voice or a whisper. Try it with an angry voice, and see if your child laughs at the disconnect between your words and the tone of your voice. Sing it, shout it; anything goes!

Goodnight, My Love

Tell a bedtime story, and, at the same time, use your finger to "draw" the story on your child's back, belly, cheek, or in the air.

Guess What?

This is a guessing game with food—eyes closed! Use foods that you know your child likes, and offer different textures and tastes. See if your child can guess what food it is. Suggest words such as "crunchy," "salty," "sour," "sweet," "soft," or "chewy," to describe each bite. This game requires a lot of trust. Let your child feed you first, to see how it feels.

Hand Hugs

Place your palms against your child's palms and interlace your fingers. Squeeze your hands together.

ALL AGES

Headstand Helper

Help your child do a handstand. What does the world look like upside down? See if your child wants to try it without you holding on.

Hello/Goodbye

Transitions can be challenging for children, especially when they must separate from their caregiver. Make up a special ritual just for hellos and goodbyes. Use eye contact and touch to support your child in feeling emotionally seen and felt.

For example, before leaving your child's preschool classroom in the morning, do your goodbye ritual. Look eye to eye and touch foreheads and palms . . . or squeeze your hands together with your child's . . . or rub noses . . . or touch elbows. Come up with something special, just for you and your child.

Performing this ritual again when you come back sends your child the message that you're still connected. You said you'd come back, and you did.

Knowing what to expect at transition times will comfort your child and make him feel safe. When children feel safe, transitions are easier.

How Tall Am I?

Use random items to measure your child, such as a spatula, a dandelion, or a sneaker. Hold the item against your child and work your way up his body, building the excitement as you count higher and higher. "Holy cow! You're four coat hangers tall!" Be sure to use an excited voice and animated gestures. Help your child find something fun to measure you with, too. (Just how many remote controls tall *is* a grownup?)

Human Pretzel

Intertwine your legs and arms with your child's, creating a human pretzel.

ALL AGES

I Hear with My Little Ear

The classic game of I Spy, with a listening twist. What do you hear with your little ear? Take turns listening for and identifying sounds around you, such as from vehicles, machines, animals, insects, crunching leaves, or raindrops.

I Love You Echoes

This is a call-and-response game in which you and your child take turns saying, "I love you." Use different silly voices, and take turns calling and copying. Try using a squeaky voice or a whisper. Try it with an angry voice, and see if your child laughs at the disconnect between the words and the tone of voice. Sing it, shout it, anything goes!

I Love You More

This listening game is a take on the children's book *Guess How Much I Love You*, by Sam McBratney and Anita Jeram. Take turns describing the size of your love:

"I love you more than all the books in the library."

"I love you more than all the candy at Halloween."

"I love you more than all the cars on this street."

I Spy

I spy with my little eye something square. Can you find it? Take turns being the one who spies and the one who guesses.

I Spy Happiness

Look for signs of happiness in the environment. These might include a wavy leaf, a tail-wagging dog, a couple holding hands, or a symbol on a billboard. Anything! Take turns finding happy things, happy people, or things that make you happy.

Kiss Fairy

Here comes the kiss fairy to kiss every part of you goodnight!

ALL AGES

Kiss Paint

Pucker up and paint your child in kisses! Plant big smooches on your child's face, arms, toes, and elbows. Let your child paint you in kisses, too.

Try using different body parts as your paint brush. For example, use your toes to paint kisses, or your thumbs. If it makes you and your child laugh, keep it up!

Magic Chef

What are we having for dinner, Magic Chef?

Ice cream sandwiches!

Lollipops and bananas!

Spaghetti with popcorn on top!

This game is great for passing time while waiting in a long line, or for redirecting your child's attention when he is nervous about an upcoming event (a doctor checkup, or preschool drop-off). Get creative, and get your silly juices flowing! When your child's silly juices are flowing, he is not stuck in his anxious thoughts anymore, and the worrisome event is much easier to face.

Make a Sound to Be Found

This game is Hide-and-Seek with a twist: Take turns hiding, and make sounds so the seeker can find you. For variation, decide on a certain type of sound, such as animal sounds or vehicle sounds. Celebrate with hugs and kisses when hider and seeker are together again!

Mystery Drop

Pick a few toys or objects and show them to your child. Tell your child to close his eyes. Then drop one object to the floor. "Can you tell which object fell, just by the sound?" Then let your child be the object picker and mystery dropper while you close your eyes.

Mystery Scent

Find some things with a nice scent, like lotion, vanilla, or perfume. See if your child can guess the smell. Don't say which scent you are using, and gently rub some on your child's arm. "What is this Mystery Scent?"

This is a good game for supporting your child in transitioning from active play to more settled play, or to mealtime or nap time.

Celebrate with hugs if your child guesses correctly. Celebrate with hugs if your child guesses incorrectly. It doesn't matter, does it? The object is to slow your child down with loving support, and to engage your child in a feeling of safe partnership with you. When your child feels this warm, happy connection with you, he or she is very likely to cooperate with your agenda.

Name That Dance Move

Have your child show you her groovy moves! Come up with new dance moves together and give them crazy names.

Name That Tune

Hum, drum, snap, or tap out a tune that's familiar to your child, and ask him to guess the song. Have your child do the same for you.

Nature Body

Stretch your arms up tall and be a tree; wave your branches toward the sky! What other nature sights can you copy with your body? You and your child can take turns pretending you are birds, flowers, or flowing water. Balance on one leg, like a flamingo. "Fly" with your arms outstretched like an owl. Experiment with different ways of moving your bodies together.

Nature Walk

Take a walk outside and talk about what you see. Take turns showing each other interesting things. Describe signs of the season, or the colors you see around you. Notice the trees and the clouds. Get curious about what your child thinks is interesting, and really listen to her when she tells you. Calm and quiet connections like this set the stage for trust and joy later.

ALL AGES

Paint the House

Use a soft makeup brush or infant hairbrush to paint your child (the house). From his roof to his basement, and all the floors in between, brush on a fresh coat of paint. Show your child how careful you are with their tickly spots, avoiding them if your child wants to relax or putting a lot of paint there if it's a silly time. Take turns, so your child gets practice with respectful touch and with being in charge. You can also try this activity in the bathtub, with shaving cream.

Be sure to admire the beautiful house when you are done!

Pat a Beat

Patting a child's back is a calming and nurturing way to use gentle touch. Make it joyful by adding a rhythm or beat. Make up your own beat or use a favorite song or nursery rhyme. Sing along, if that seems fun to you. Vary your tempo, based on your child's mood and what your child responds to. You can play your beat on different body parts, like gentle pats to the head, or harder pats to the knees. Take turns patting beats on each other, and, for a twist, see if one of you can make up a beat and the other can copy it—on each other's bodies, of course.

Pick 1

What would you rather be? Pick one: elephant or gorilla?

Pen or pencil?

Football or basketball?

What would you rather have:

A rocket ship or a submarine?

Treehouse or tent?

What would you rather do:

Be the fastest runner or the fastest swimmer?

Reality is not a problem in this game. Think of any two choices and let your child take a pick. Take turns, and see if your child can think of a choice for you.

Power Postures!

Stand in front of a mirror with your child, or stand face to face. Stand strong and tall, like a superhero. Flex your amazing muscles! Admire your child's powerful body, and see how many ways she can pose. Show your child how to use her body to radiate confidence, bravery, and strength.

Pretzel Hug

Link elbows, as if you were going to twirl in a circle together. Squeeze your elbows tight to seal in the love. Twirl in a circle, if that seems fun!

Rescue Hugs

Dramatically "rescue" your child from different "dangers." "There's a wild elephant coming? Oh, no! I'll save you!" Scoop up your child in a great big hug and carry her to safety. Save your child from lions, tigers, and bears. Save her from a mouse or a baby and see how she laughs. You can also use real dangers, such as fire or "bad guys," but be sure to emphasize the playfulness and your total confidence in "saving" your child.

Role Reversal

Your child gets to tuck you into bed, hugging and kissing you good-night. Then you do the same for your child.

Also try Role Reversal when you and your child are stuck in a power struggle. Let your child "help" you brush your teeth, then you help her with hers.

Sandwich Hug

Two people (other than your child) are the "bread," and your child is the filling. The bread people gently and playfully hug the filling. Have your child decide what kind of filling to be (Peanut butter? Turkey?), so that she has a feeling of control over the game.

ALL AGES

Scent Art

Use scented lotions or essential oils to make your child's artwork smell good. Add cinnamon or vanilla to homemade play dough. Use scented markers. Trade sniffs of your favorite smells. Sprinkle lavender essential oil on uncooked rice for a soothing sensory experience.

Secret Handshake

Create a secret handshake with your child, your own special connection that nobody else knows. Use it anytime, especially when separating or coming together (such as daycare drop off and pick up). Let your child to be in charge of when to do the secret handshake, or plan together about when you'll use it.

This activity allows for quick and effortless moments of connection and touch throughout the day. For inspiration, watch basketball stars before their games start, or when they celebrate a big play or a win. Their routines can be pretty elaborate. A simple fist bump and then wiggling fingers is fine, too!

Secret Sound

Create a secret code word or sound, and a silly thing to do when you hear it. "Today's secret sound is a cat's meow. If you hear me meow, stick out your tongue." Or "The secret word today is 'pizza.' If you hear the word 'pizza,' give me a high five." Once your child understands this silly game, she can help come up with the next code word and action. Use this game to give your child permission to do something that usually is considered rude, such as sticking her tongue out, wiggling her fingers in her ears at you, or making a mean face. That makes it especially fun to do!

Silly Salad

Let's make a silly salad! Everyone around the table takes a turn saying what she would like in the silly salad. What do you want to put in your salad? Eggs? Sparkles? Monkeys? The sillier the better! Don't forget the silly salad dressing!

Simon Says: Balance

Call out poses for your child that are challenging and require balance. Feel free to add making silly sounds or animal imitation a part of the game.

"Simon says: Hop on one foot while clucking like a chicken."

"Simon says: Bend down to your toes, then jump up."

This activity starter takes a classic game and makes the focus all about the challenge of balance. Simon says: "Enjoy!"

Sing Along

Sing a soothing song in a relaxing tone using your child's name instead of the real lyrics. Use a classic children's song, or try it with a popular song from the radio.

"The eensy weensy *Jonathon* went up the water spout. Down came the rain and washed *Jonathon* right out!"

Smell and Guess

Fill a small container with different scented items, like a cotton ball sprayed with perfume, an orange peel, a dryer sheet, or a leaf. Close your eyes and guess which thing your child is holding in front of your nose. Try this with random things like the TV remote, a pencil, or a toy. You'll be surprised by the unique smells of everyday objects!

Smell Hunter

Just like the old saying, "Stop and smell the roses," pause to enjoy this moment, right here and right now. What do you smell? Find things all around you that have a scent. Can you smell the lotion on your arms, or the paper in a magazine? Find real things to smell by going on a "smell hunt." Or pretend you smell dinosaurs or monkeys.

Star in My Jar

Create a calm-down jar with your child. Find an old jar with a lid. Use glitter glue, glitter, food coloring, warm water, and small toys and trinkets (like hearts, stars, smiley faces, etc.). Add half a bottle of glitter glue to the jar, then add warm water and your trinkets. Next, add food

ALL AGES

coloring and glitter. Last, seal the lid on with hot glue or Crazy Glue.

Shake, shake, shake and watch the glitter spin! Set the jar down and watch everything slowly settle to the bottom. Give a kiss when you spot a heart, and a hug for every star. Make up similar games that are unique to the toys you put in the jar.

Strike a Pose

Take turns holding a pretend camera and posing for the perfect shot. The photographer can give prompts, like "Say cheese" or "Show me goofy!" These silly images will only remain in your memory, so let go and have fun!

Super-Special Grocery Game

When you're at the grocery store, find something interesting or unusual to take home to eat. The food doesn't have to be fancy or require much special preparation (unless that sounds like fun to you!). Maybe you'll pick a variety of apple that you've never tried before, or a new kind of canned soup. The point is the joy of searching together, and the excitement of sharing something new.

Taco Night

Take a trip around the world with your child—through food! Pick a country and talk about the foods that are common there, then make one of those foods for dinner. Or find a kids' book that features food, and make that. It can be as easy as noticing that there is a picture of a pizza in a book your child likes; then, next time you eat pizza, bring out that book. Good books that feature food are *Dragons Love Tacos*, by Adam Rubin and *Curious George and the Pizza Party*, by Margret and H.A. Rey.

Telephone

Take turns whispering into each other's ears and repeating what you heard. The whispers can be words, phrases, or sounds—the sillier the better. "Underwear grows on trees!" "Broccoli is yummy!" "My dog is a bus driver!" Use with younger students.

Texture Talk

Crunchy, crumbly, creamy, mushy—there are so many ways to describe how food feels in your mouth! Tune in to these sensations, and help your child do the same. While you're talking about food textures, you're also sharing the experience of eating with your child. This helps your child to feel your loving attention in a brand new way, and helps bring some connection to mealtime.

Throw a Kiss

Another activity for sharing some long-distance love. Kiss your palm, then wind up and make a big throw. Make sure your child is looking at you, and add some excitement and energy, especially when your child throws his kiss back at you. Jump with joy and rub that spot on your cheek where his kiss hit the mark.

Thumb Kiss

Press your thumb against your child's thumb and make a big smooching sound. Or use your thumb to press kisses all over your child's face and body. Seal them in with kissing sounds and smiles.

Thumb Wiggles

Face your child and clasp your child's fingers with yours, thumbs on top. Take turns "catching" each other's wiggly thumb in this silly version of thumb wrestling. Make your thumb wiggle in fright, or make it wild and wavy. There are no rules, and no winners or losers in this game.

Tickle Time

"Guess what time it is? Tickle Time!" Wiggle your fingers and approach your child, building the suspense as you get closer and closer. Call out a body part: "Tickle belly!" Then tickle, tickle, tickle and repeat! Take turns being the tickler, or have your child tell you which body part he wants you to tickle.

Pay close attention to your child's cues in this game. Tickling can feel overwhelming for some people, and doesn't always feel fun. Stop

ALL AGES

if your child seems scared, or if you can't tell whether your child is laughing because it's fun or because he's nervous.

Treasure Hunt

Go on a scavenger hunt and find "treasures" all around you. In a doctor's waiting room, the treasures might be a checker, a tissue, and a paperclip. Outdoors, you might find pinecones or dandelions or blades of grass. Explore the different ways these treasures feel, by touching them with your hands, or placing them against your arm or cheek. Use lots of descriptive words, like bumpy, knobby, smooth, prickly, scratchy, soft. Take turns finding, showing, and feeling. You could also try this with eyes closed; ask your child to guess which treasure it is just by feel.

Tug o' War

Your child is the rope, and you are "battling" with him/her to move to the next thing. You and your child can take turns being the "rope."

Twirly Hugs

Wrap your arms around you child's back (near the waist) and twirl in a circle.

Wheelbarrow Race

Hold your child's feet while he balances on his hands, with his body parallel with the floor. You've got yourself a wheelbarrow. See if you can walk your wheelbarrow around the room!

Keep in mind that younger children might not be strong enough to hold themselves up for very long. Just be playful and see what happens. Try to work together as a team. You can even trade places, and have your child try to hold your legs up!

Winky Blinky

Sit face to face with your child and ask her to copy your winks and blinks (and also your squints, wide-open eyes, and eyes looking up, down, left, and right)!

Wishes for the World Game

Send out positive thoughts to the world! What do you and your child wish for others? That everyone has love? That all children have yummy food to eat? Take turns making wishes for others. Your child might wish that everyone has a special blankie, or the same spoon that he has; it's not important that each wish be realistic, honorable, or deeply felt. Just enjoy the process of thinking about others, and get your child in the practice of compassion. Even if your child's wishes for the world are all about potties or panda bears, that's OK! You can feel free to wish for world peace, or just embrace the silliness and wish for bubble gum for everyone!

Wizard Kiss

Your finger becomes a magic wand. Kiss the tip of your finger and then wave it in the air. Abracadabra! Use your finger wand to cast your kiss onto your child! This kiss is handy when your child isn't right next to you. For example, if your child has taken a seat on the school bus and is looking at you out the window, cast a finger-spell her way!

ALL AGES